Evolution:
Good Science?

Exposing the ideological nature
of Darwin's theory

Dominic Statham

DayOne

© Day One Publications 2009
First printed 2009

ISBN 978–1–84625–170–2

British Library Cataloguing in Publication Data available

Unless otherwise indicated, Scripture quotations in this publication are from the **New International Version** (NIV), copyright ©1973, 1978, 1984, International Bible Society. Used by permission of Hodder and Stoughton, a member of the Hodder Headline Group. All rights reserved.

Published by Day One Publications
Ryelands Road, Leominster, HR6 8NZ
☎ 01568 613 740 FAX 01568 611 473
email—sales@dayone.co.uk
web site—www.dayone.co.uk
North American—e-mail—sales@dayonebookstore.com
North American—web site—www.dayonebookstore.com

Cover design by Wayne McMaster
Printed by Gutenberg Press, Malta

I enjoyed this book very much! It is both well written and illustrated in a style that clearly explains the problems with evolution—its history and current popularity—and offers a cogent alternative. I recommend it to anyone interested in the origins controversy.

Dr. R. Terry Spohn, Professor of Biology and Associate Director of Creation Studies, Liberty University, Lynchburg, Virginia, USA

This book presents an excellent summary of the origins debate. As an experienced engineer, Dominic Statham is well qualified to take on the task of analysing a mass of disputed evidence and making conclusions that are fair and justified.

Stuart Burgess, Professor of Design and Nature, University of Bristol

Thⁱhis book presents an excellent summary of the origins debate. As an experienced engineer, Dominic Statham is well qualified to take on the task of analysing a mass of disputed evidence and making conclusions that are fair and justified.

The title is very appropriate because there is often more faith than science when it comes to believing the theory of evolution. Many evolutionists believe in the spontaneous generation of life despite the fact that no one has been able to reproduce it in the last sixty years in the laboratory. And many evolutionists believe that gene mutations can give rise to new information and new structures despite the fact that no one can give any clear examples of this happening in the natural world.

Dominic Statham has found many telling quotes from evolutionists. If evolution is a fact of science, why do so many evolutionists express doubts about evolution in their own area? The quotations show that the media are wrong when they say that the scientific community accepts evolution as an undisputed fact of science.

The book also addresses the crucial question of whether or not evolution is compatible with the Bible. There can be a strong temptation to accept the theory of evolution in order to appear to be a friend of science. But accepting evolution involves accepting an ideology which is fundamentally against God and the Bible. Even if evolution were possible, it is not compatible with what the Bible reveals about the creation account or the character of God. Scripture reveals that God had only to speak the word in order to create the world.

I am sure that this excellent book will be a great help to many people who want to know the truth about origins.

Stuart Burgess
Professor of Design and Nature, University of Bristol

As a schoolboy, I was introduced to the theory of evolution, as a scientifically proven fact, in the religious education classes. No doubt the teacher, who was not a scientist, had been assured that evolution had been proven and had honestly sought to help us reconcile this aspect of 'modern science' with what the Bible tells us about our origins. Not long after, as a university student in the early 1980s, I was introduced to a very different view, this time by an eminent scientist. He was Professor E. H. Andrews, Head of Department of Materials at Queen Mary College, University of London. Professor Andrews was speaking at a meeting of the Christian Union and his address was entitled, 'Is Evolution Scientific?' It quickly became apparent that, on scientific grounds alone, he did not accept the theory of evolution and believed that much evolutionary thinking failed to apply good scientific method.

In the decades since, much more has been said and written about the weaknesses of evolution theory and, contrary to the propaganda of some organizations active in promoting evolutionary beliefs, the leading scientists who have rejected evolution are neither ignorant nor poorly qualified. In fact, many of them, having doctorates from major universities, and having spent many years researching the subject, have very detailed knowledge of the issues. Indeed, it is my experience that, in many cases, they are better informed about evolution theory than some evolutionists. It is to these that I am greatly indebted, and, in as much as the reader may find this book helpful, it is primarily because of their hard work. Particularly to be commended for their meticulous and pioneering efforts are the Institute for Creation Research, Answers in Genesis and Creation Ministries International. The web addresses for these and other creationist organizations are given below.[1]

I do not generally write on subjects that are already well covered, and there is now much excellent material relating to the creation/evolution debate available in books and on the web. However, when I began my investigations, I was unable to find a short summary of the arguments presented in support of evolution, together with the reasons why these arguments are rejected by a growing number of well-informed scientists. It is this, primarily, that I have attempted to provide.

Preface

Researching this subject has been one of the greatest eye-openers of my life.

Dominic R. Statham

May 2009

Note

1 Institute for Creation Research: icr.org; Answers in Genesis: answersingenesis.org; Creation Ministries International, creationontheweb.com; Biblical Creation Society: biblicalcreation.org.uk; Biblical Creation Ministries: biblicalcreationministries.org.uk; Creation Science Movement: csm.org.uk; Truth In Science: truthinscience.org.uk; Biology Study Group: creationbiology.org.

Contents

Introduction

According to the scientists put before the general public week in, week out, 'evolution is a fact'. The evidence, they argue, that man evolved from inanimate matter, over many hundreds of millions of years, is so compelling that no reasonable scientist disputes this. Such is the opinion, for example, of Douglas Futuyma, who is Professor of Ecology and Evolution at the State University of New York. In his book *Evolutionary Biology*, he states that evolution 'is a fact, as fully as the fact of the earth's revolution about the sun'.[1] According to the US National Academy of Sciences, 'the scientific consensus around evolution is overwhelming'.[2] Without doubt, this statement would be supported by Dr Richard Pike, Chief Executive of the Royal Society of Chemistry, who in April 2006 demanded that children be taught Darwin's theory of evolution as fact.[3] In the same month, the UK National Academy of Science issued 'a statement on evolution, creationism and intelligent design'.[4] In it, they claimed,

One of the most important advances in our knowledge has been the development of the theory of evolution by natural selection. Since being proposed by Charles Darwin nearly 150 years ago, the theory of evolution has been supported by a mounting body of scientific evidence. Today it is recognised as the best explanation for the development of life on Earth from its beginnings and for the diversity of species. Evolution is rightly taught as an essential part of biology and science courses in schools, colleges and universities across the world.

The process of evolution can be seen in action today, for example in the development of resistance to antibiotics in disease-causing bacteria, of resistance to pesticides by insect pests, and the rapid evolution of viruses that are responsible for influenza and AIDS. Darwin's theory of evolution helps us to understand these problems and to find solutions to them.

Coming from some of the world's top scientists, such statements lead many to understand that the theory of evolution is indeed scientifically proven, and that to believe otherwise is simply to bury one's head in the sand. Accordingly, 'Christian fundamentalists', who hold to the account of creation in the Bible, are assumed to ignore science or to be 'pseudo-scientists' who do not really understand science. But is this really true? Are the arguments presented in support of evolution really so compelling? In the following chapters, I shall demonstrate that there are in fact many serious problems with the theory of evolution that are rarely presented to students or to the general public. Moreover, I shall argue that we can reasonably accept the Bible's explanation for life *and* be true to science.

Notes

1 **Douglas J. Futuyma,** *Evolutionary Biology* (2nd edn.; Sunderland, MA: Sinauer Associates, 1986), p. 15.
2 National Academy of Sciences, *Teaching about Evolution and the Nature of Science* (Washington DC: National Academy Press, 1998), p. 56.
3 **Jonathan Petre,** 'Creationism Gathers Strength at Conference', *Daily Telegraph*, 22 April 2006, at telegraph.co.uk.
4 April 2006 at: royalsociety.org/news.asp?year=&id=4298.

Part 1

Clarifying principles

What is Darwin's theory of evolution?

A s a young man, Charles Darwin travelled extensively. Having accepted the position of Naturalist on board HMS *Beagle*, he made, during the years 1831 to 1836, an intensive study of plant and animal life across the Southern Hemisphere. Among his many observations, he was particularly struck by the way species are often confined to particular geographical areas. Around the Galápagos archipelago, for example, he discovered that many similar but distinct

Fig. 1 Islands of the Galápagos archipelago

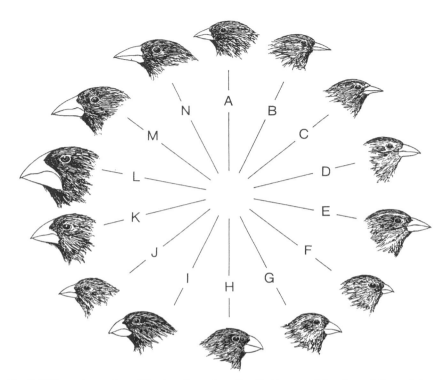

Fig. 2 Different species of finches found on the Galápagos Islands and Cocos Island
© Jody F. Sjogren, 2000. Used by permission.

Each species is adapted to its own niche. The shape and strength of the finches' bills, as well as the muscles attached to them, are suited to the type of food they eat. The cactus finch, the woodpecker finch, the cocos finch and the warbler finch all have long and pointed bills. These birds probe flowers or foliage for food. Their bills are also good for spearing insects. The ground finch and the cactus finch have bills that are deep at the base. Their bills are good at crushing hard seeds and other hard food. (Peter Grant, *Ecology and Evolution of Darwin's Finches* (Princeton: Princeton University Press, 1986)).

A: Sharp-beaked ground finch B: Cocos Island finch   C: Warbler finch

D: Mangrove finch   E: Woodpecker finch   F: Small tree finch

G: Medium tree finch   H: Large tree finch   I: Vegetarian finch

J: Small ground finch   K: Medium ground finch   L: Large ground finch

M: Large cactus finch   N: Cactus finch

species of plants and animals inhabit the different islands (Fig. 1). Perhaps the best-known example is the thirteen different species of Galápagos finches. Of particular significance is that each appears to be specially adapted to its environment, for example, having a beak shape most suited to the kind of food available on the island on which it is found. Moreover, the similarities and differences between them are such that they can be arranged in a morphological sequence (Fig. 2). With good reason, Darwin wrote of these birds that it was as if 'one original species had been taken and modified for different ends'.[1]

In 1859, Darwin published his famous book, *The Origin of Species*, in which he presented what became known as his 'Special and General Theories of Evolution'. His Special Theory held that, just as new species can be produced by processes of *artificial selection* (that is, selective breeding), so they can and do arise through processes of *natural selection*. Hence, for example, one species of bird can give rise to many different species of bird; one species of dog can give rise to many different species of dog. His General Theory was an extension of his Special Theory, arguing that the same processes that give rise to new species can also, over millions of years, cause one kind of animal to change into another; for example, a fish into an amphibian or a reptile into a bird. Darwin's Special Theory of Evolution (STE) is also referred to as *micro-evolution*, *adaptation* or *speciation*, and his General Theory of Evolution (GTE) as *macro-evolution*.

Darwin's theory holds that natural variation in a population is constantly tested for advantage by the environment. Beneficial variation, such as the ability to collect food more effectively or to move with more agility, confers upon an organism a capacity to survive better and, in 'the struggle for life', it is 'naturally selected', living longer and reproducing more. Through heredity, the new, beneficial characteristics are passed to subsequent generations and spread throughout the population. Over time, he argued, these accumulate, gradually changing one species into another.

Although Darwin believed he understood the process of natural selection, he had no explanation for the cause of variation. In the 1940s, scientists began to formulate theories that would explain variation through genetics, and discoveries in molecular biology, particularly DNA in the 1950s, further refined these ideas. Hence, the Neo-Darwinian Theory (NDT) was born, which held that the variation was caused by *random genetic mutations*. DNA acts like a computer program, controlling how organisms grow and function. If the program changes, then the form or function of the organism will change. In order to reproduce, an organism copies its own DNA, so as to be able to pass this down to the next generation. Copying errors (called mutations) occur, which change the program and give rise to variation in the offspring.

Hence, according to neo-Darwinian theory, *natural selection* gives direction to variation caused by *genetic mutation* and, over millions of years, causes speciation within an animal kind and evolution of one animal kind into another. This evolutionary sequence is generally claimed to be single-celled organisms ⇨ invertebrate sea creatures ⇨ vertebrate fish ⇨ amphibia ⇨ reptiles ⇨ birds and mammals. Hence, neo-Darwinian theory supposedly explains how single-celled organisms evolved into all the animals we see today. Similar explanations are given for the alleged evolution of plants.

Furthermore, just as neo-Darwinian theory seeks to explain how single-celled organisms could develop into plants and animals, so *chemical evolution* seeks to explain how simple chemicals could combine through natural, random processes to form these first single-celled organisms. Since nineteenth-century scientists had little knowledge of molecular biology, Darwin himself could only speculate vaguely as to how this might have occurred. He conceived of a 'warm little pond with all sorts of ammonia and phosphoric salts, light, heat and electricity' in which the first living organisms might have formed.[2] The modern theory is similar, holding that the random shuffling of chemicals on the earth's surface many millions of years ago led to the forming of basic organic compounds, which accumulated in 'primordial oceans'. Supposedly, these organic compounds were then assembled, by random (or unknown) processes, into proteins and nucleic acids (DNA), which then combined to form the first self-replicating cells.

Hence, through chemical evolution, followed by random genetic mutations and natural selection, ordinary chemicals supposedly became people. This is sometimes called the theory of *molecules-to-man evolution*.

Notes

1 **Charles Darwin,** *The Voyage of the Beagle* (1845; 1959, London: J. M. Dent & Sons), p. 365. As a point of history, it should be noted that Darwin's speculations relating to the Galápagos finches were made after he returned from his voyage, not when he visited the islands in 1835. Furthermore, most historians are agreed that the finches played only a minor role in the formulation of his evolutionary ideas, and that his observations of other animals featured much more prominently in his thinking (**Jonathan Wells,** *Icons of Evolution*, ch. 8 (Washington DC: Regnery Publishing, 2000)). However, since they provide such a good example of the proliferation of species, the finches are often given special prominence in the presentation of his theory.

2 **N. Barlow,** *Autobiography of Charles Darwin* (London: Collins, 1958), pp. 235–237.

Part 2

Evidence presented in support of evolution and a creationist response

The fossil record

For many, the fossil record is still the strongest argument that can be made in support of the theory of evolution. They believe that the sedimentary rocks were laid down gradually, over many millions of years, and that entombed in the various rock layers are the remains of plants and animals that lived at various times in history (Fig. 3). Since the lowest rock strata contain only invertebrates (and no birds or mammals, for example), they are understood to represent 'the age of invertebrates', when only creatures of this form lived on the earth. Rock strata above these are believed to represent 'the age of fishes', when vertebrates first appeared. Similarly, strata above these are seen to represent 'the age of amphibia', 'the age of reptiles' and 'the age of mammals'. Hence, it is argued, the rocks contain a chronology of the development of life, with 'simple' invertebrate sea creatures found in the lowest strata, more complex fish in strata above them, yet more complex amphibia above the fish, reptiles above the amphibia, and birds and mammals above the reptiles. Supposedly, then, in the fossil record, we see the evolutionary progression, invertebrate sea creatures ⇨ vertebrate fish ⇨ amphibia ⇨ reptiles ⇨ birds and mammals.

But is this interpretation of the sedimentary rocks and the fossils they contain necessarily correct? Do general observations of the rocks support this interpretation? Since nobody was around to see how the rocks were formed, explanations for their existence are really only hypotheses, rather than facts. If we are to be scientifically rigorous, we must test these hypotheses. Specifically, we must ask,

- If the fossils do indeed show the sequence of the development of life, what sort of fossils would we expect to find?
- Do studies of sedimentary rocks confirm the belief that they were laid down slowly, over millions of years?

The answer to the first question is that we would expect the fossil record to be characterized by 'transitional forms'. For example, we would expect to find fossils showing the gradual change of one species into another. We would also expect to find creatures with 'transitional structures'. For

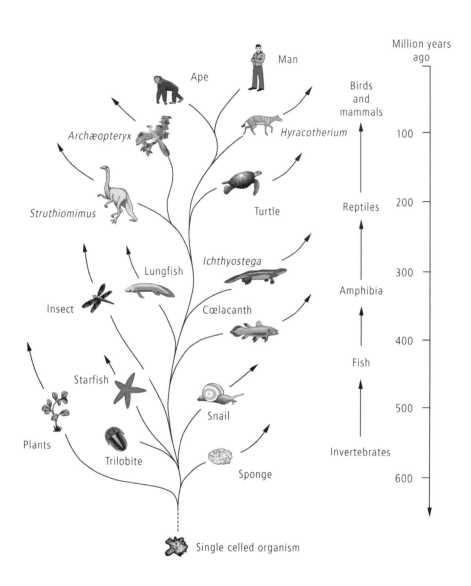

Fig. 3 Alleged evolutionary tree together with the supposed ages of the rock strata in which each kind is first found. © John Lewis 2009

example, if invertebrates had evolved into vertebrates, we would expect to find fossils of creatures that had partly-formed backbones. If reptiles had evolved into birds, we would expect to find fossils of creatures with legs that were becoming wings and scales that were becoming feathers. It is here that we find one of the greatest difficulties facing evolutionists, because forms that might be argued to be genuinely transitional are very rare. Indeed, because of the lack of such 'transitional fossils', Charles Darwin himself, in his *Origin of Species*, admitted that the fossil record was, perhaps, 'the most obvious and gravest objection' to his theory.[1] Other evolutionists are equally clear about the lack of transitional fossils. David Kitts, who was Professor of Palaeontology at the University of Oklahoma, comments, 'Despite the bright promise that paleontology provides a means of "seeing" evolution, it has presented some nasty difficulties for evolutionists, the most notorious of which is the presence of "gaps" in the fossil record. Evolution requires intermediate forms between the species and paleontology does not provide them.'[2] Professor David Raup, formerly Curator of the Field Museum of Natural History, Chicago, is similarly candid:

Instead of finding the gradual unfolding of life, what geologists of Darwin's time, and geologists of the present day, actually find is a highly uneven or jerky record; that is, species appear in the sequence very suddenly, show little or no change during their existence in the record, then abruptly go out of the record. And it is not always clear, in fact it's rarely clear, that the descendants were actually better adapted than their predecessors. In other words, biological improvement is hard to find.[3]

Dr Colin Patterson FRS, who was the senior palaeontologist of the British Museum of Natural History, replying to the question as to why he had not included any pictures of transitional forms in his book *Evolution*, wrote,

If I knew of any, fossil or living, I would certainly have included them. You suggest that an artist should be used to visualize such transformations, but where would he get the information from? I could not honestly provide it, and if I were to leave it to artistic licence, would that not mislead the reader? I wrote the text of my book four years ago.

If I were to write it now, I think the book would be rather different. Gradualism is a concept I believe in, not just because of Darwin's authority, but because my understanding of genetics seems to demand it. Yet Gould and the American Museum people[4] are hard to contradict when they say there are no transitional fossils. As a palaeontologist myself, I am much occupied with the philosophical problems of identifying ancestral forms in the fossil record. You say that I should at least show a photo of the fossil from which each type of organism was derived. I will lay it on the line—there is not one such fossil for which one could make a watertight argument.[5]

One explanation put forward by evolutionists to explain the lack of transitional fossils is that evolution took place very rapidly, and in small, isolated groups. Consequently, it is argued, the evolving organisms were too few and existed for too short a period for their transitional forms to be captured in the fossil record. Professor Stephen J. Gould and Dr Niles Eldredge, for example, believed that the lack of transitional fossils indicated that new species developed through what they described as *punctuated equilibrium*. According to this theory, organisms in large populations remain substantially unchanged for long periods (perhaps millions of years), but then evolve rapidly (perhaps over just a few tens of thousands of years). Supposedly, this occurs in response to sudden changes in the environment and in small groups that have broken away from the main population. Hence, it is argued, the large, stable populations are captured in the fossil record, but not the emerging new species. However, since it is a theory based on the *absence* of intermediates, it really *assumes* rather than *establishes* an evolutionary interpretation of the rocks and fossils. It also requires a mechanism which will drive evolution at a very fast pace, whereas most theories of evolution rely on long ages to bring about change through random mutations, very few of which will be favourable.[6]

Moreover, theories such as punctuated equilibrium consider only the problem of the lack of intermediates at the level of species. Hence, they fail to address the greater difficulty of the lack of transitional fossils between the higher taxonomic groups—that is, between families, orders, classes, and phyla. Here, there is a conspicuous absence of fossils documenting the evolution of radically new structures, such as joints, jaws, legs or wings.

Indeed, not only are fossil intermediates of such structures not found, it is, in some cases, even difficult to imagine what they might have looked like. Professor Gould comments, 'The absence of fossil evidence for intermediary stages between major transitions in organic design, indeed our inability, even in our imagination, to construct functional intermediates in many cases, has been a persistent and nagging problem for gradualistic accounts of evolution.'[7] Similarly, Professors David Raup and Steven Stanley argue, '... the origins of most higher categories are shrouded in mystery; commonly new higher categories appear abruptly in the fossil record without evidence of transitional ancestral forms.'[8]

Speaking of the fossils found in the Cambrian rocks, which supposedly document the first appearance of the major groups of organisms living today, the palaeontologist Professor Euan Clarkson states, '... transitional or linking forms are absent ... the geological record gives no indication of such relationships ... But what the fossil record does give is many examples of the "instantaneous" origin of new structural plans.'[9] Also speaking of the Cambrian fossils, Oxford University Zoologist Professor Richard Dawkins openly admits, 'It is as though they were just planted there, without any evolutionary history.'[10]

Arguments to the effect that the evolutionary links between the fossils have simply not yet been found have become progressively less tenable over the years, as armies of palaeontologists have searched and searched for them in vain. According to Professor Raup,

Darwin's general solution to the incompatibility of the fossil evidence and his theory was to say that the fossil record is a very incomplete one ... Well, we are now about 120 years after Darwin and the knowledge of the fossil record has been greatly expanded ... ironically, we have even fewer examples of evolutionary transition than we had in Darwin's time. By this I mean that some of the classic cases of Darwinian change in the fossil record, such as the evolution of the horse in North America, have had to be discarded or modified as a result of more detailed information.[11]

The problem is particularly serious in respect of fossils of sea creatures, as there are tens of millions of these lying in drawers and display cabinets all over the world. Evidence of evolution from single-celled organisms to invertebrates is conspicuously absent, as is the evidence of evolution from invertebrates to vertebrates. As Dr Duane Gish (former Senior Vice-President of the Institute for Creation Research) argues,

All of the complex invertebrates appear fully formed, without a trace of ancestors or transitional forms linking one to another. Many millions of years would have been required for their origin by evolutionary processes. Billions times billions of their fossils lie entombed in rocks all over the world, including all kinds of soft-bodied creatures. Even many published reports of the discovery of fossils of microscopic, single-celled, soft-bodied organisms have appeared in scientific journals. If evolution is true, the rocks should contain billions times billions of fossils of the ancestors of the complex invertebrates. *Yet, not one has ever been found.* It is simply physically impossible to have millions of years of evolution, producing a vastly diverse collection of complex invertebrates, without leaving a trace. Even more convincing, if that can be said, is the total absence of intermediates between invertebrates and fishes, and the total absence of ancestors and transitional forms for each major class of fishes.[12]

So widespread and systematic is the lack of transitional fossils that some evolutionists have been driven to postulate the most remarkable ideas to explain it. For example, Professor Richard Goldschmidt, who was a leading geneticist at the University of California, Berkeley, proposed the theory of *macro-mutation*, which holds that genetic mutations caused radical changes in anatomy in one step. According to this, the first bird would have hatched from a reptilian egg, for example.[13] Goldschmidt's idea has enjoyed some high-profile support in recent years, namely from Professor Gould, who argued that the marked absence of fossil transitional forms, and the limited functionality of transitional structures (such as a partly formed joint), are insurmountable objections to the Neo-Darwinian Theory of gradual change.[14] Most evolutionists regard Goldschmidt's theory as quite implausible, however.

Claims of transitional fossils are of course made from time to time. One of the most commonly cited examples is *Archaeopteryx*, which was a bird with some features similar to those of reptiles (Figs 4 and 5). For example, it had a long bony tail, teeth, and claws on its wings. But is this really a

Fig. 4 Fossil of *Archaeopteryx*
Photo by Jim Amos, Science Photo Library

Fig. 5 Artist's impression of *Archaeopteryx* © John Lewis 2009

According to ornithologists Professors Richard Prum and Alan Brush, '*Archaeopteryx* offers no new insights on how feathers evolved, because its own feathers are nearly indistinguishable from those of today's birds'.[15] This, together with the fact that its wings are similar in size and shape to those of modern birds, presents strong evidence that *Archaeopteryx* was a flying bird, rather than a reptile becoming adapted for flight. Furthermore, it had a bony sternum (breastbone), indicating that it had strong wing muscles.

More recent candidates for reptile/bird transitional forms include *Sinosauropteryx*, *Protarchaeopteryx*, *Caudipteryx*, *Microraptor* and *Velociraptor*. *Sinosauropteryx* appeared to have a coat of filamentous structures that some claimed were the beginnings of feathers. According to Professor Alan Feduccia of the University of North Carolina, however, these are more likely to be the remains of collagen fibres that reinforced the animal's skin.[16] Professor Feduccia also argues that *Protarchaeopteryx* and *Caudipteryx* were, in fact, flightless birds, rather than forms transitional between dinosaurs and birds. These were probably descended from ancestors that could fly. Significantly, both have the characteristic digits (fingers) of a bird, which are quite different from those of the theropod dinosaurs from which they supposedly evolved. The three digits of the theropod hand are 1, 2 and 3, digits 4 and 5 being reduced during embryonic development, while the three digits of the bird hand (wing) are 2, 3 and 4, digits 1 and 5 being reduced or resorbed during embryonic development.[17] The 2–3–4 digital pattern of the hand of *Microraptor* suggests that it might also be understood to be a bird. *Velociraptor* may well have been a feathered dinosaur. However, the existence of such creatures does not establish the truth of evolution, as this requires examples of characteristics which are in a state of transition. Characteristics which are fully formed, and shared with other organisms, do not provide evidence that one kind of animal has turned into another. Similarly, organisms that are less adapted for flight, because they have lost characteristics possessed by their flying ancestors, provide evidence of *de*volution (that is, degeneration), not evolution.

convincing transitional form? It had fully developed feathers all over its body, together with bones that most likely supported muscles for powered flight. To be 'transitional', a fossil must show characteristics or structures which are *partly formed*, such as reptilian scales on the way to becoming feathers, or fish fins on the way to becoming limbs. Moreover, if evolution were true, we would expect the fossil record to be *characterized* by transitional forms. Instead, we find only a few questionable examples.

Lest there still be any doubt in the reader's mind as to whether or not the fossil record really supports the theory of evolution, I conclude with the words of ardent evolutionist and Oxford University Zoologist Dr Mark Ridley:

… the gradual change of fossil species has *never* been part of the evidence for evolution. In the chapters on the fossil record in the *Origin of Species* Darwin showed that the record was useless for testing between evolution and special creation because it has great gaps in it. The same argument still applies … In any case, no real evolutionist, whether gradualist or punctuationist, uses the fossil record as evidence in favour of the theory of evolution as opposed to special creation.[18]

Figs 6 and 7 (opposite) Sand pumped in a water slurry onto a beach on the Gold Coast, Australia

This sand settled in thin layers. From *Creation,* creationontheweb.com. Used by permission.

Secondly, do studies of sedimentary rocks confirm the belief that they were laid down slowly over millions of years? Traditionally, evolutionists have argued that the many thin layers from which the rocks are composed are clear evidence of this. But do such layers *necessarily* indicate gradual deposition of sediments? In his book *Refuting Evolution*, Dr Jonathan Sarfati gives a number of examples of both observations and experiments that show this not to be the case.[19] For example, when large quantities of sand were pumped in a water slurry onto a beach on the Gold Coast, Queensland, Australia, it was observed that the sand settled in thin layers, rather than an amorphous mixture (Figs 6 and 7). When Mount St Helens in Washington erupted in 1980, fine layers of ash, up to 7.6 metres thick, were produced by pyroclastic flows in a matter of hours (Fig. 8). Experiments in which sedimentary rocks are broken down into their constituent particles and then laid down again in water slurry show that the sediments resettle in layers, even recreating the appearance of the original laminated rocks from which they came. These and other experiments suggest that it is not possible

Fig. 8 Metres of finely layered rock at Mount St Helens, Washington, USA
The central section was produced in just hours on 12 June 1980. Note the person for scale. Photo by Steven. A. Austin.

to deduce the rate of sedimentation simply by studying the rock layers.[20] Furthermore, fossils showing intricate details of soft body parts are sometimes found bridging many layers—could soft body parts have remained in a perfect state of preservation while waiting to be covered slowly by sediments over many years?

Another argument traditionally used in support of slow rates of sedimentation is that long periods of quiet water conditions are required for the deposition of mud. Supposedly, then, where thousands of alternating thin layers of sand and clay are found, such rock formations must have been laid down over many years. Similarly, it is argued that the immense thickness of some mudstone rocks cannot have formed quickly, because the rate of sedimentation would have been too slow. However, recent experiments conducted by Juergen Schieber, an Associate Professor of Geological

Fig. 9 Polystrate tree fossils, Cumberland Mountains, Tennessee, USA
These are very common and are often found in coal mines. Some polystrate trees pass vertically up through several layers of coal, between which are layers of sedimentary rock. Could trees have remained in such a preserved state while waiting to be entombed in sediments and organic material over many thousands of years?[21] © Don R. Patton 2008

Sciences at Indiana University, have shown that mud *can* deposit from fast-flowing water.[22] In a report in *Science* magazine, he argues,

Our observations do not support the notion that muds can only be deposited in quiet environments with only intermittent weak currents ... Many ancient shale units, once examined carefully, may thus reveal that they accumulated in the manner illustrated here, rather than having largely settled from slow-moving or still suspensions. This, in turn, will most likely necessitate the reevalution of the sedimentary history of large portions of the geologic record.[23]

In his book *The Young Earth*, Dr John Morris presents strong evidence that most of the sedimentary rocks were laid down very rapidly, through massive flooding, rather than through gradual processes. For example,

- The presence of 'polystrate fossils', where, for example, a single fossilized tree passes vertically up through several coal seams and

Fig. 10 Deformation of Tapeats Sandstone, Carbon Canyon, Arizona
Note the people for scale. Had this rock been hard when bent, we would expect to see evidence of the elongation of its sand grains, or the cement which bound the grains together broken and recrystallized. Such features, however, are not found. See John Morris, *The Young Earth* (Green Forest, AR: Master Books, 2007), p. 111. © Paul Garner 2004

metres of sedimentary rock, is powerful evidence of very rapid accumulation of sediments and organic material (see Fig. 9). Such fossilized trees are *common* and are often found, for example, in coal mines.

- In many mountainous areas, rock strata over a thousand metres thick have been tightly bent through earth movements without cracking or heating, indicating that they were still soft when deformed (Figs 10 and 11). If these rocks had been laid down over millions of years, it is most likely that the lower strata would have hardened and could not have been bent without cracking.
- Fossil graveyards, where billions of creatures are buried and

Fig. 11 Tight folding of rocks at Split Mountain, California
Note the person for scale. Photo by Steven A. Austin.

fossilized very close together, must have been created through sudden deposition of enormous amounts of sediment.

- The rarity of erosion features and fossilized soil layers between rock strata is inconsistent with their being separated by millions of years (Figs 12, 13 and 14).

- The lack of bioturbation[24] within rock layers is inconsistent with many thousands of years of slow deposition. Bioturbation can remove almost all traces of a layered sedimentary structure in less than twenty years.[25]

The belief that many rock strata and geologic features were produced through catastrophic action rather than slow, gradual processes is not restricted to creationists. Although most geologists do not believe in a young earth, an increasing number argue that most sedimentary rocks were laid down very rapidly. One of these 'catastrophists', Professor Derek Ager, who was Head of Department of Geology and Oceanography at Swansea University, wrote,

Fig. 12 Typical rock layers (Badlands, South Dakota)
Why are the tops of these rocks now exposed to the weather so eroded and uneven, but not the rock strata below, supposedly exposed to the elements millions of years ago?
© Tony Colter. Reproduced by iStockphoto Extended Licence

… I maintain that a far more accurate picture of the stratigraphical record is of one long gap with only very occasional sedimentation … The hurricane, the flood, or the tsunami may do more in an hour or a day than the ordinary processes of nature has [sic] achieved in a thousand years … Given all the millennia we have to play with in the stratigraphical record, we can expect our periodic catastrophes to do all the work we want of them … In other words, the history of any one part of the earth, like the life of a soldier, consists of long periods of boredom and short periods of terror.[26]

The argument that canyons and deep ravines can only be produced by slow erosion over millions of years is now known to be false. In 1926, when

Fig. 13 Coconino Sandstone overlaying the Hermit Formation, Bright Angel Trail, Grand Canyon
The contact is an astonishingly flat surface over a large area, with no evidence of prolonged erosion or soils, even though the rock types are supposedly separated by around 10 million years. © Paul Garner 2004

engineers diverted water away from irrigation channels near Walla Walla, Washington, this cut a canyon 450 m long, 35 m wide and 35 m deep in six days.[27] Canyon Lake George, Texas, which measures 2.5 km long and 24 m deep, was produced by water overflowing from the nearby lake in 2002 in just three days.[28] Large mudflows have also been observed to create similar features.[29] Moreover, it is now known that the eroding power of fast-flowing water is sufficient to rip up even hard igneous rock.[30]

Another argument in support of the sedimentary rocks being millions of years old comes from radiometric dating. This is often done, for example, by analysing 'igneous intrusions', where molten rock has intruded into sedimentary rocks (after the sedimentary rocks have formed) and subsequently cooled and solidified. But how reliable are radiometric dating methods? Many people have been led to believe that these provide

Fig. 14 Coal seams visible in a road cut near Price, Utah
Observe the sharp contacts between the coal and the adjacent layers. If the rock strata were laid down over thousands of years, why is there no evidence of erosion? (See icr.org/article/521.) © Institute for Creation Research. Used by permission. Photo by Dr John Morris.

highly accurate and dependable results. This is not so, however, and the literature is replete with examples of obviously wrong dates.[31] The following are some interesting examples.

- Samples from a lava dome on Mount St Helens were analysed at the Geochron Laboratories, Cambridge, Massachusetts. The lava, which was known to be around ten years old, was dated by the potassium-argon method as being between 0.34 and 2.8 million years old.[32]
- Miners in the Crinum coal mine, Central Queensland, Australia, found pieces of wood entombed in basalt lava. The wood was dated at around 45,000 years old by the carbon-14 method, but the basalt was dated at around 45 million years old by the potassium-argon method.[33]
- Zircons extracted from granite-type rock and dated at around 1.5 billion years by the uranium-lead method were found to have amounts of retained helium (also produced by this decay process) consistent with an age of only 6,000 years.[34] Had the rock really been many millions of years old, nearly all the helium would have leaked out of the samples.

The most likely explanation for these anomalies is that the assumptions behind the methods are invalid. For example, with the potassium-argon method, it is generally assumed that there is no argon present in the lava when it solidifies, which is highly questionable, as shown, for example, by the results from the samples taken from Mount St Helens. All the methods assume a constant half-life of radioactive decay; however, the analyses of the zircons suggest that decay rates were much faster in the past. The question must be asked, 'If the assumptions are seen to be unreliable when dating rocks of known age (such as those at Mount St Helens), how can we rely on them when dating rocks of unknown age?'

Interestingly, the best-known radiometric dating method, using carbon-14, actually provides some of the strongest evidence that the sedimentary rocks are not millions of years old. Contrary to popular belief, carbon-14 is not used to date material that is believed to be millions of years old. This is because it has a relatively short half-life and occurs only in very small quantities. Consequently, the theoretical limit for carbon-14 dating is only around 100,000 years, as beyond this, any remaining carbon-14 would be undetectable. So, when carbon-14 is found in coal or other fossils, it suggests that the sedimentary rock in which they are buried is less than 100,000 years old.[35]

Because of the anomalies found when using radiometric dating methods, it is clear that there are factors which are not understood. In our opinion, their acceptance as proving the rocks to be very old is derived much more from the evolutionary paradigm, which *requires* millions of years, than from rigorous scientific practice.

According to the traditional geological interpretation of the sedimentary rocks, fossils of dinosaurs must be millions of years old. However, a partially fossilized *Tyrannosaurus rex*, supposedly around 65 million years old, was recently found to contain the protein collagen, together with soft, flexible tissues, including bone and blood vessels.[36] Tests subsequently showed strong evidence that these blood vessels contained the remains of blood cells with preserved traces of the protein haemoglobin.[37] It stretches credibility a very long way to believe that these organic substances could last for millions of years. The discovery of well-preserved DNA in plant fossils is another indication that the rocks that contain them are not millions of years old, because, due to the speed at which it breaks down, DNA is unlikely to last more than 10,000 years.[38]

Other arguments traditionally presented in support of old ages are also increasingly coming into question. The process of fossilization does not necessarily take thousands of years, as many have been taught, as there are examples of artefacts that have been petrified in a few hundred years or fewer. The seventeenth-century Venetian chapel of Santa Maria de Salute was built on wooden pilings to reinforce its foundations. These have now turned to stone.[39] In fact, wood in the form of trees and posts has been known to petrify in fewer than a hundred years.[40] A felt hat was fossilized in around fifty years in a mine in Tasmania (Fig. 15).[41] Are millions of years required to form coal? Coal has been produced in a laboratory, under conditions similar to those that might be expected in a geological formation, in much less than a year.[42] Stalactites and stalagmites are traditionally understood to take many thousands of years to form, supposedly indicating that the caves in which they are found must be very old. However, stalactites up to 30 cm long are sometimes found on bridges,

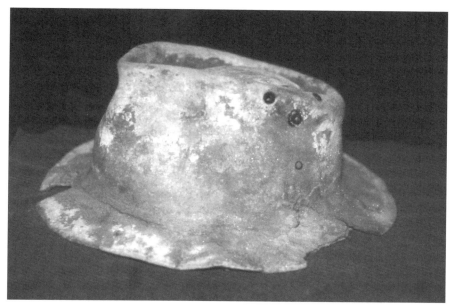

Fig. 15 Fossilized felt hat found in a mine in Tasmania
From *Creation*, creationontheweb.com. Used by permission.

and stalactites in caves have been known to grow a number of centimetres in a matter of days.43 In October 1953, *National Geographic* magazine published a photograph of a bat that had fallen onto a stalagmite in a cave in New Mexico. The stalagmite had grown at such a rate that the bat did not have time to decompose before it was covered.44 Just because some stalactites and stalagmites are seen to be growing very slowly today, it does not follow that they have always grown at this rate.

An alternative explanation for the sedimentary rocks, and for the billions of fossils they contain, is the Bible's account of a worldwide flood and the associated destruction of all (non-waterborne) life except for that saved by God in the ark (Genesis 6–8).45 There is much evidence for such a global catastrophe. Fossils of sea creatures are found covering all the continents, including mountainous areas such as the Himalayas.46 Even Mount Everest is capped by limestone containing marine fossils. There are extensive fossil 'graveyards' where billions of creatures are buried in close proximity to one another.[47] These are seen, for example, in the Old Red Sandstone stretching from Loch Ness in Scotland to the Islands of Orkney. This rock formation, which is 150 km across and over 2.5 km thick, contains many fossils showing many signs of catastrophic burial, with billions of fish contorted and contracted, as though in convulsion, and bearing the marks of a violent death. In the Silawik Hills north of Delhi, rich beds are found crammed with fossils, including a 7-m-long tortoise, a species of elephant with tusks 3 m long and 1 m in circumference, pigs, rhinoceroses, apes and oxen. In Central Burma (Myanmar), deposits are found containing the remains of mastodon, hippopotamuses and oxen, along with thousands of fossilized tree trunks. Many other examples could be cited.[48] Rock layers can be traced all the way across continents;[49] for example, the Tapeats Sandstone and the Redwall Limestone of Grand Canyon stretch across the USA up into Canada, and even across the Atlantic Ocean. The chalk beds of England can be traced all the way across Europe to the Middle East. In some cases, the most catastrophic processes would have been required to erode millions of tons of sediment and transport it long distances.[50] The Coconino Sandstone of Arizona, for example, appears to have originated in the northern USA and Canada.

In these 'flood models', the fossil sequence found in the rocks can be understood to indicate the order in which the plants and animals were buried in the sediments deposited by the floodwaters. Sea creatures, and particularly those living on the bottom of the ocean, would have been buried first, followed by plants and animals living in or close to water, such as amphibia. Land animals would have been buried last, either because they lived far from lakes or seas, or because they fled the rising floodwaters, with the more mobile creatures being caught and buried later than the less mobile. According to this view, the rock strata can be argued to represent different ecological or 'biogeographic' zones, rather than different eras of history.[51] There are other factors arising from a massive water catastrophe that could have contributed to the pattern of fossils seen in the rocks. For example, the sorting action of water would tend to result in smaller, denser creatures being buried beneath larger, less dense creatures. Fossilized shellfish, for example, can be seen to follow this pattern. Some Flood models include massive earth movements (also required to raise the continents after the Flood). These could have caused large areas of land to sink, along with the flora and fauna living on them, and subsequently be destroyed or covered with Flood sediments and fossils.[52] Some fossil deposits were probably laid down by water catastrophes that occurred some years after the Genesis Flood. In fact, there is much discussion among creationist geologists as to where the Flood/post-Flood boundary should be drawn. Most are agreed, however, that the geological record points to catastrophic processes in recent history, rather than gradual processes over millions of years.

The popular understanding of the rocks and fossils is that they provide a record of the evolution of life. That is, they are believed to show the gradual change, over millions of years, of 'primitive' single-celled organisms into highly complex organisms such as birds and mammals. If this were true, it would be expected that the fossils would be characterized by transitional forms, documenting both the change from one species to another and the development of radically new structures, such as joints and wings. Instead, the record is characterized by 'sudden appearance' of both new species and new body structures. This suggests that an alternative interpretation of the rocks and fossils should be sought.

As will be seen in the following chapters, creationists accept that, within strict limits, species can and do change. For example, there is strong evidence that animals (and plants) can adapt to different environments, even to the extent that they can, justifiably, be called new species. There is no evidence that one kind of animal can change into another—for example, a reptile into a mammal—but there is good scientific reason to believe that species are not strictly fixed in their form. This is entirely consistent with the Bible, as all the species of land animals living today must be descended from the limited number of animals that were saved in the ark. Moreover, if speciation took place after the flood, it would be expected that it also occurred prior to the Flood. The question should then be asked, 'If species can and do change, why is this so rarely captured in the fossil record?' Here, the biblical account of history provides an answer. According to this, most of the sedimentary rocks were laid down rapidly,

What is a kind?

According to the book of Genesis, God created plants and animals 'according to their kinds' (Genesis 1:11–12, 21, 24–25). Biblical creationists understand this to mean, firstly, that organisms have always belonged to separate groups that have never been related to one another, and, secondly, that there are limits to the variation possible within a kind. Hence, the process of speciation could never cause fish to become reptiles, for example, or apes to become men. The question might be asked, 'What is a kind?' Dr Carl Wieland suggests, 'Groups of living organisms belong in the same created kind if they have descended from the same ancestral gene pool'[53] and, according to Dr Todd Wood, a created kind can be said to 'contain a complete set of organisms that share continuity among themselves but are discontinuous with all other organisms'.[54]

In practice, this means that a biblical kind might be classified as a genus, or, in some cases, a family. Creation scientists recognize that a more systematic approach to understanding kinds is required, and this work is ongoing. See creationbiology.org; **D. A. Robinson,** (ed.), *Baraminology '99* (Baraminology Study Group, 1999) and **M. Helder,** (ed.), *Discontinuity: Understanding Biology in the Light of Creation* (Baraminology Study Group, 2001).

over the course of the year-long Flood. Hence, for most organisms, there simply would not have been enough time for speciation to occur.

It is important to note that the biblical model does not predict that *no* transitional fossils will be found. Rather, it predicts that these will be rare, and will show only limited degrees of change. Clear sequences of transitional fossils may be found between species (the lowest taxonomic level), but not between higher groups, such as fish, amphibia, reptiles and mammals. The occasional discovery of transitional fossils may be explained in three ways. Firstly, if pre-Flood speciation occurred, in which the original species was not replaced by the new species but continued to exist alongside it, this could have been captured in the sedimentary rocks laid down during the flood. Secondly, where the generation time of an organism is very short, there may have been time for speciation to occur during the one-year Flood. Thirdly, a record of the speciation of organisms with both shorter and longer generation times may be seen in sedimentary rocks laid down after the Flood. This would be seen higher up the geological column.[55] Moreover, these rocks may provide clues to the history of animal and human life following the recolonization of the world after the Flood.[56]

According to the Bible, God created plants and animals as distinct kinds (Genesis 1:11–12, 21, 24–25). This would suggest that the process of speciation acts within strict limits and cannot cause one kind of plant or animal to change into another. Hence, for example, a reptile could 'speciate' into another reptile, but not into a mammal. Consequently, it would be expected that there would be significant 'gaps' in the pattern of life, and that all organisms could be categorized into separate, non-overlapping groups. Again, this prediction is realized in the fossil record, as transitional forms between major body structures are markedly absent.

Australopithecus afarensis (A. afarensis)

The currently popular alleged link between apes and humans is one of the Australopicethines, *Australopithecus afarensis* (meaning 'Southern Ape of the Afar region' of Ethiopia), often referred to as 'Lucy'. (Strictly speaking, 'Lucy' was the specimen found by Donald Johanson in 1974.)

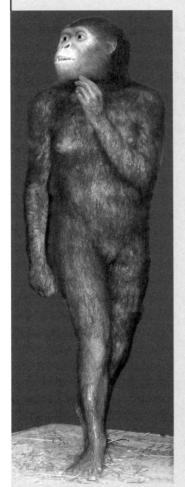

The model shown in Fig. 16 depicts *A. afarensis* as having an ape's head on what is essentially a human body. It appears to be entirely comfortable either standing or walking on two legs. But to what extent does this reflect the fossils that have actually been found? According to David Menton, formerly Associate Professor of Anatomy, Washington University School of Medicine, the creature is more likely to have been a tree-dweller and knuckle-walker. It had finger and toe bones more curved than those of many apes, and shoulder joints suitable for hanging from branches, indicating that its natural habitat was among the trees. It also had bones to lock the wrists, consistent with it adopting a knuckle-walking, bent-over posture rather than a human-like bipedal gait.[57]

According to Charles Oxnard, Professor of Human Anatomy and Human Biology, University of Western Australia, '... the australopithecines known over the last several decades ... are now irrevocably removed from a place in the evolution of human bipedalism ... All this should make us wonder about the usual presentation of human evolution in introductory textbooks ... It is now being recognized widely that the australopithecines are not structurally closely similar to humans ...'[58]

Fig. 16 Model of A. Afarensis ('Lucy') at St Louis Zoo, Missouri
Photo by Ivan Burgener

The fossils, however, show that the toes were long and curved, not human-like. Furthermore, there is no fossil evidence showing that the *A.*

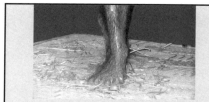

Figs 17 and 18 Shape of feet and hands on the St Louis Zoo model Photo by Ivan Burgener

afarensis big toe was aligned with the foot (as on the model), rather than sticking out to the side as with living apes. The hands on the model are also misleading, appearing small and human-like, with straight finger bones. In fact, speaking of the hands of A. *afarensis*, Stern and Susman comment, 'one is struck by the morphologic similarity to apes.'[59]

Moreover, the chest of A. *afarensis* was funnel-shaped, like that of modern apes, not barrel-shaped as with humans, and the hands hung almost to the knees.

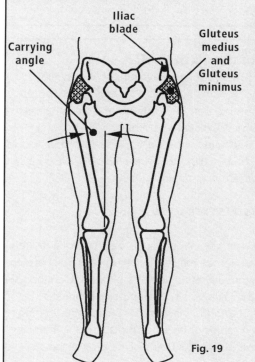

Iliac blade

Carrying angle

Gluteus medius and Gluteus minimus

Fig. 19

WHY IS *A. AFARENSIS* TO BE BIPEDAL?

The evidence that caused Donald Johanson (the discoverer of 'Lucy') to declare it to have stood upright and walked habitually on two legs was its 15° carrying angle (Fig. 19). Humans have a carrying angle of 9°, which places their feet close together, almost under their centre of gravity, enabling them to walk naturally and easily on two legs. Gorillas and chimpanzees have a carrying angle of 0°, placing their feet apart and away from their centre of gravity. Consequently, when they walk on two legs, they throw their weight from side to side in an awkward movement. However, orangutans are not bipedal and yet, like humans, they have a carrying angle of 9°. As with orangutans, A. afarensis may have had a high carrying angle primarily to help it walk along narrow tree branches.

It should be admitted that other characteristics of A. afarensis anatomy, such as the shape of its pelvis, would have enabled it to walk more effectively on two legs than apes seen today.[60] However, it appears that this would have been more of a 'waddle' and quite different from the striding gait of humans.[61] Along with many others, researchers at the State University of New York have concluded that A. afarensis' bipedality was characterized by a 'bent-hip, bent-knee' movement.[62] It is even questionable as to whether A. afarensis could have stood still and upright (as suggested by the St Louis Zoo model) without losing its balance. This is because the iliac blades of the pelvis do not wrap as far around the sides of the body as they do in true bipeds (humans). Consequently, the muscles attached to them (the gluteus medius and gluteus minimus) would have been less effective in maintaining side-to-side balance.[63] According to Professor Oxnard, the nature of A. afarensis' bipedality was *not intermediate* between apes and humans, *but unique.*[64]

Radioisotopes and the age of the earth (RATE)

In 2005, the results of an eight-year, $1·25 million research project were published by the RATE group.[65]

These detailed the findings of scientists from the Institute of Creation Research (icr.org) and the Creation Research Society (creationresearch.org) who had sought to investigate the claim that radiometric dating conclusively proved the earth and its sedimentary rocks to be many millions of years old. They discovered much evidence that contradicts this view, two aspects of which are summarized here.

HELIUM RETENTION IN ZIRCON CRYSTALS EXTRACTED
FROM GRANITE-TYPE ROCKS

Zirconium silicate crystals (zircons), which contain uranium, are frequently found in granite-type rocks. The uranium, being radioactive, decays through a number of steps into lead, at a known rate. Assuming that the rates of decay are constant, an estimate can be made of the length of time the decay has been in process by measuring the amounts of uranium and lead in the sample. This then provides an indication of the age of the rock. Another indication of age can be obtained by measuring the amount of helium present. This is because helium is a by-product of the same decay processes, and the amount of helium that would have been produced can be calculated, along with the amount that would have leaked out of the sample by diffusion. In other words, knowing the rates of helium production and subsequent loss, an estimate of the age can be calculated from the amount retained. Clearly, if the assumptions and measurements are all correct, the age obtained from the uranium-lead analysis should be similar to that obtained from the helium analysis.

The RATE team analysed samples obtained by drilling into 'basement' rock in New Mexico, up to 4·3 km deep. Using the uranium-lead analysis, these were dated at 1·4 billion years. The helium analysis, however, yielded a figure of 6,000 years. This suggests that the assumption of constant decay rates, upon which all radiometric dating is based, is flawed, and that rates of decay have been much faster in the past. If this is correct, then many radiometric 'dates', which allegedly prove the earth and its sedimentary rocks to be many millions of years old, are wrong.

UBIQUITOUS CARBON-14

Carbon-14 is another radioactive element, which decays into nitrogen at a known rate. However, in this case, the measured decay rate is very fast—in just 5,730 years (its 'half-life'), 50 per cent will have decayed away. In fact, assuming a constant half-life, a lump of carbon-14 as massive as the earth would all have decayed away in less than a million years. Consequently, when carbon-14 is found in a sample, if we assume a constant rate of decay, we must conclude that the sample can be only thousands of years old, not millions of years old.

There are many reports of carbon-14 being found in organic material supposedly millions of years old. These include fossils, petrified wood, shells, whale bone, coal, oil and natural gas. Those who hold to the view that these samples are genuinely millions of years old argue that they must have been contaminated with substances carrying carbon-14 within the last 100,000 years. The RATE team, however, undertook carbon-14 dating in a material which, due to its hardness, is very unlikely to become contaminated—diamonds. These, again, were found to contain carbon-14, indicating that they are not millions of years old, as 'ancient earth' geologists maintain.

Notes

1 **Charles Darwin,** *The Origin of Species* (Oxford: Oxford University Press, 1998), p. 227.
2 **David B. Kitts,** 'Paleontology and Evolutionary Theory', *Evolution*, 28 (1974), p. 467.

3 **David Raup,** 'Conflicts between Darwin and Paleontology', *Field Museum of Natural History Bulletin*, 50/1 (1979), pp. 23–29.

4 That is, Professor Steven J. Gould of Harvard University and Dr Niles Eldredge of the American Museum of Natural History. See **Stephen Jay Gould,** 'Evolution's Erratic Pace', *Natural History*, 86/5 (1977), p. 14; and **Niles Eldredge,** *Time Frames: The Rethinking of Darwinian Evolution and the Theory of Punctuated Equilibria* (London: Heinemann, 1986), p. 144.

5 **Colin Patterson,** cited in **Luther D. Sunderland,** *Darwin's Enigma: Fossils and Other Problems* (Green Forest, AR: Master Books, 2002), pp. 101–102.

6 **Walter J. ReMine,** *The Biotic Message* (St Paul, MN: St Paul Science, 1993), pp. 220–221.

7 **Stephen Jay Gould,** 'Is a New and General Theory of Evolution Emerging?', *Paleobiology*, 6/1 (1980), pp. 119–130.

8 **Raup** and **Stanley,** *Principles of Paleontology* (San Francisco: W. H. Freeman & Co., 1971), p. 306.

9 **Euan N. K. Clarkson,** *Invertebrate Palaeontology and Evolution* (4th edn.; London: Blackwell Science, 1998), p. 45.

10 **Richard Dawkins,** *The Blind Watchmaker* (1986; 2006, London: Penguin), p. 229.

11 **Raup,** 'Conflicts between Darwin and Paleontology'.

12 **Duane Gish,** *Evolution: The Fossils still Say NO!* (El Cajon, CA: Institute for Creation Research, 1995), p. 81.

13 **Richard Goldschmidt,** cited in **Duane Gish,** *Creation Scientists Answer their Critics* (El Cajon, CA: Institute for Creation Research, 1993), pp. 142–144.

14 **Stephen J. Gould,** 'The Return of Hopeful Monsters', *Natural History*, 86/6 (1977), pp. 22–30.

15 **Richard Prum** and **Alan Brush,** 'Which Came First, the Feather or the Bird?', *Scientific American* (March 2003), pp. 84–93.

16 **Alan Feduccia,** 'Latest Study: Scientists Say No Evidence Exists that Therapod Dinosaurs Evolved into Birds', University of North Carolina News Release 477, 10 October 2005, at: unc.edu/news/archives.

17 **Alan Feduccia et al.,** 'Do Feathered Dinosaurs Exist? Testing the Hypothesis on Neontological and Paleontological Evidence', *Journal of Morphology*, 266/2 (2005), pp. 125–166; at: www3.interscience.wiley.com/cgi-bin/home.

18 **Mark Ridley,** 'Who Doubts Evolution?', *New Scientist*, 90 (June 1981), pp. 830–832.

19 **Jonathan Sarfati,** *Refuting Evolution* (Green Forest, AR: Master Books, 2000), ch. 8; see creationontheweb.com/content/view/3837.

20 Richard Milton, *Shattering the Myths of Darwinism* (1st edn.; Rochester, VT: Fourth Estate, 1997), pp. 77–78.

21 In Lancashire, a fossil tree was found that was 11.5m high and still standing in its living position. In Gilboa, USA, a whole forest was uncovered, with trees up to 12m high. (See **Derek V. Ager,** *The Nature of the Stratigraphical Record* (3rd edn.; Chichester: John Wiley & Sons, 1993), pp. 65–66, and **Derek V. Ager,** *The New Catastrophism* (Cambridge: Cambridge University Press, 1993), p. 49.)

22 Tas Walker, *Mud Experiments Overturn Long-Held Geological Beliefs*, 9 January 2008, at: creationontheweb.com.

23 Juergen Schieber et al., 'Accretion of Mudstone Beds from Migrating Floccule Ripples', *Science*, 318 (December 2007), pp. 1760–1763.

24 Bioturbation is a process in which sediments are mixed up by organic activity, for example, by plant roots, worms and the burrowing activities of shellfish.

25 John Morris, *The Young Earth* (Green Forest, AR: Master Books, 2007), ch. 8.

26 Derek V. Ager, *The Nature of the Stratigraphical Record* (3rd edn.; Oxford: John Wiley & Sons, 1993), pp. 52, 80, 141.

27 John Morris, 'A Canyon in Six Days', *Creation*, 24/4 (2002), pp. 54–55, at: creationontheweb.com; answersingenesis.org.

28 Shaun Doyle, 'A Gorge in Three Days!', 10 October 2007, at: creationontheweb.com.

29 Steven Austin, *Mount St Helens: Explosive Evidence for Catastrophe* (DVD; available from the Institute for Creation Research, California).

30 Ager, *The Nature of the Stratigraphical Record*, p. 77; **David Catchpoole,** 'Beware the Bubble's Burst: Increased Knowledge about Cavitation Highlights the Destructive Power of Fast-Flowing Water', 24 October 2007, at: creationontheweb.com; **Steven Austin,** (ed.), *Grand Canyon: Monument to Catastrophe* (El Cajon: CA: Institute for Creation Research, 1994).

31 Don Batten, (ed.), *The Answers Book* (6th edn.; Acacia Ridge, Queensland: Answers in Genesis, 2004), ch. 4; **John Woodmorappe,** *The Mythology of Modern Dating Methods* (El Cajon, CA: Institute for Creation Research, 1999); **Andy McIntosh,** *Genesis for Today* (3rd edn.; Leominster: Day One, 2006), pp. 209–219.

32 Steven Austin, 'Excess Argon within Mineral Concentrates from the New Dacite Lava Dome at Mount St Helens Volcano', *TJ* (Journal of Creation), 10/3 (1996), pp. 335–343, at: answersingenesis.org; creationontheweb.com.

33 Andrew Snelling, 'Radioactive "Dating" in Conflict!', *Creation*, 20/1 (1997–1998), pp. 24 27, at: answersingenesis.org; creationontheweb.com.

34 Don DeYoung, *Thousands not Billions* (Green Forest, AR: Master Books, 2005), ch. 4.

35 Ibid., ch. 3; **Andrew Snelling,** 'Stumping Old-Age Dogma: Radiocarbon in an "Ancient" Fossil Tree Stump Casts Doubt on Traditional Rock/Fossil Dating', *Creation*, 20/4 (1998), pp. 48–51, at: creationontheweb.com; **Andrew Snelling,** 'Radiocarbon Ages for Fossil Ammonites and Wood in Cretaceous Strata near Redding, California', *Answers Research Journal* 1 (2008), pp. 123–144, at: answersingenesis.org.

36 **Mary Schweitzer** and **Tracy Staedter,** 'The Real Jurassic Park', *Earth* (June 1997), p. 55–57; Mary Schweitzer et al., 'Analyses of Soft Tissue from *Tyrannosaurus Rex* Suggest the Presence of Protein', *Science*, 316 (2007), pp. 277–280; **Shaun Doyle,** 'Squishosaur Scepticism Squashed: Tests Confirm Proteins Found in *T. Rex* Bones', CMI, April, 2007, at: creationontheweb.com.

37 **Carl Wieland,** 'Sensational Dinosaur Blood Report!', *Creation*, 19/4 (1997), pp. 42–43, at: creationontheweb.com; answersingenesis.org; **Carl Wieland,** 'Evolutionist Questions CMI Report: Have Red Blood Cells Really Been Found in *T. Rex* Fossils?', 25 March 2002, at: creationontheweb.com; 'Evolutionist Questions AiG Report', at: answersingenesis.org.

38 **Carl Wieland,** 'DNA Dating: Positive Evidence that the Fossils Are Young', *Creation*, 14/3 (1992), p. 43, at: creationontheweb.com; answersingenesis.org.

39 Cited in **Andrew Snelling,** '"Instant" Petrified Wood', *Creation*, 17/4 (1995), pp. 38–40, at: answersingenesis.org; creationontheweb.com.

40 Ibid.

41 '"Fossil" Hat', *Creation*, 17/3 (1995), p. 52, at: creationontheweb.com/content/view/1694; answersingenesis.org.

42 **Ryoitchi Hayatsu et al.,** 'Artificial Coalification Study: Preparation and Characterisation of Synthetic Macerals', *Organic Geochemistry*, 6 (1984), pp. 463–471; **Elizabeth Pennisi,** 'Water, Water, Everywhere: Surreptitiously Converting Dead Matter into Oil and Coal', *Science News*, 20 February 1993, pp. 121–125.

43 *Arizona Highways*, January 1993, pp. 4–11.

44 **Mason Sutherland,** 'Carlsbad Caverns in Color', *National Geographic*, 104/4 (1953), pp. 433–468.

45 More accurately, the Genesis Flood wiped out all land animals that breathed through nostrils (Genesis 7:22).

46 **Andrew Snelling,** 'High and Dry Sea Creatures', *Answers*, 3/1 (2007), pp. 92–95, at: answersingenesis.org.

47 **Richard Milton,** *Shattering the Myths of Darwinism* (1st edn.; Rochester, VT: Park Street Press, 1997), pp. 90–95.

48 **Andrew Snelling,** 'The World's a Graveyard', *Answers*, 3/2 (2008), pp. 76–79, at: answersingenesis.org.

49 Andrew Snelling, 'Transcontinental Rock Layers', *Answers*, 3/3 (2008), pp. 80–83, at: answersingenesis.org.

50 Paul Garner, *The Grand Canyon: Evidence for the Global Flood*, lecture to the Edinburgh Creation Group, 2008; at: edinburghcreationgroup.org.

51 Kurt P. Wise, *Faith, Form and Time* (Nashville, TN: Broadman & Holman, 2002), chs. 12 and 13; **Todd C. Wood** and **Megan J. Murray,** *Understanding the Pattern of Life* (Nashville, TN: Broadman & Holman, 2003), pp. 188–191.

52 John Woodmorappe, 'A Diluviological Treatise on the Stratigraphic Separation of Fossils', *Creation Research Society Quarterly*, 20/3 (1983), pp. 133–185.

53 Dr Carl Wieland, 'Variation, Information and the Created Kind', *TJ* (Journal of Creation), 5/1 (1991), pp. 42–47.

54 Dr Todd Wood, 'A Baraminology Tutorial with Examples from the Grasses (Poaceae)', *TJ* (Journal of Creation), 16/1 (2002), pp. 15–25.

55 Kurt P. Wise, 'Punc. Eq. Creation Style', *Origins*, 16/1 (1989), pp. 11–24, at: grisda.org.

56 Paul Garner, *The New Creationism* (Darlington: Evangelical Press, 2009), ch. 16.

57 D. Menton, *Lucy: She's No Lady*, DVD, 2006, at: answersingenesis.org/video/ondemand.

58 Charles Oxnard, *The Order of Man: A Biomathematical Anatomy of the Primates* (New Haven: Yale University Press, 1984), p. 332.

59 J. Stern and **R. Susman,** 'The Locomotor Anatomy of Australopithecus Afarensis', *American Journal of Physical Anthropology,* 60 (1983), pp. 279–317.

60 Matthew Murdock, 'These Apes Were Made for Walking', TJ (*Journal of Creation*) 20/2, pp. 104–112.

61 Christine Berge, 'How Did the Australopithecines Walk? A Biomechanical Study of the Hip and Thigh of Australopithecus afarensis', *Journal of Human Evolution,* 26 (1994), pp. 259–273.

62 Roger Lewin, *Human Evolution: An Illustrated Introduction* (5th edn.; Oxford: Blackwell Publishing, 2005), pp. 133–134.

63 Murdock, 'These Apes Were Made for Walking'.

64 Charles E. Oxnard, *Fossils, Teeth and Sex: New Perspectives on Human Evolution* (Hong Kong: Hong Kong University Press, 1987), pp. x, 121, 227–232.

65 Larry Vardiman, Andrew Snelling and Eugene Chaffin, (eds.), *Radioisotopes and the Age of the Earth,* vols 1 and 2 (El Cajon, CA: Institute for Creation Research, 2000). A popular-level version is also available: **Don DeYoung,** *Thousands Not Billions* (Green Forest, AR: Master Books, 2005).

'It is observed today'

Within the scientific community, among both evolutionists and creationists, the processes of adaptation and speciation are almost universally held to be fact. Darwin's contention that all the Galápagos finches were descended from one original species is, for example, almost certainly correct. This is because the circumstantial evidence that such processes have occurred in the past and still occur today is strong, being seen in clear anatomical and genetic sequences. Other examples of adaptation, such as the emergence of bacteria resistant to antibiotics and insects resistant to pesticides, are also generally acknowledged, by both creationists and evolutionists, to be fact. But do examples of adaptation and speciation demonstrate processes that could give rise to the evolution of one kind of animal into another?

Fundamental to the process of 'molecules-to-man' evolution is the requirement to progressively increase genetic information. Genetic information is the set of instructions, encoded in DNA molecules, which is used to grow a new organism. It consists of 'letters' (called *nucleotides* or *bases*) that make up 'words' and 'sentences' that define the structure of the plant or animal—how to make a leaf, root, heart, lung, or brain, for example. The theory of evolution maintains that, starting with chemicals in a 'primordial soup' that had no genetic information, gradually, over millions of years, primitive self-replicating chemical systems arose as the original genetic information materialized. From them, increasingly complex, living organisms supposedly evolved by continuously reproducing themselves in more and more complex forms as genetic information continued to grow. Allegedly, this ultimately gave rise to the indescribably complex and information-rich genomes found in modern plants and animals.[1]

Although many evolutionists accept that there are difficulties explaining the origin of the genetic information leading to the first biological cell,[2] they argue that processes that could enable living organisms to generate new genetic information are observed in nature. This is because DNA copying errors (mutations), which occur when organisms reproduce, are occasionally seen to give rise to beneficial change. A more rigorous consideration of these claims, however, reveals a different picture. This is because, almost without exception, the known examples of beneficial copying errors have been seen to occur through *reduction* or *loss* of pre-existing function. A good example is the way some bacteria have gained resistance to the antibiotic penicillin. Bacteria that have a resistance to low, naturally occurring levels of penicillin can develop resistance to the high levels of penicillin prescribed by doctors by a mutation of the gene that controls the amount of penicillinase they produce (penicillinase is the enzyme that resists penicillin). The mutation destroys the bacteria's ability to control the production of penicillinase (a loss of function) and, consequently, they overproduce this and thereby 'evolve' extra resistance. Many other examples are known of beneficial mutations in bacteria that arise through loss of function.[3] Another way bacteria may gain resistance to an antibiotic is through gene transfer. Here, the gene for resistance is transferred from bacteria that already have a natural resistance to the antibiotic. Clearly, in neither case is there an increase in function—in the one, there is loss of function and, in the other, a transfer of a function (or information) that already exists. Insects are also known to acquire resistance to insecticides through loss of function.[4]

Evolution requires mutations that *increase* information and function, and these are very, very rare. In fact, some question whether any have been observed at all. The biophysicist Dr Lee Spetner was a fellow of Johns Hopkins University who taught information and communication theory and specialized in information in DNA. Having studied the theory of evolution for over thirty years, he concluded, '… of all the mutations studied since genetics became a science, not a single one has been found that adds a little information.'[5] Here Dr Spetner was referring to the fact that all the mutations he had studied had led to genes becoming less specific in their function.[6] Continued degeneration of gene specificity would lead to the death of organisms, not their evolutionary improvement.

Another way new genetic information is defined is in terms of the capacity to produce new organs or structures—the building blocks of macro-evolutionary change. Again, the geneticist Dr John Sanford of Cornell University is equally clear: 'It must be understood that scientists have a very sensitive and extensive network for detecting information-creating mutations—most scientists are diligently keeping their eyes open for them all the time … Yet I am still not convinced there is a single, crystal-clear example of a known mutation which unambiguously created information.'[7]

If evolution were true, information-increasing mutations must have occurred often in the past, in order to generate the enormous amounts of genetic information now existing in nature—in all the plants, animals and other living organisms. In fact, much, much more information would have had to be generated than is contained within all these genomes. This is because, in order to contribute to evolutionary change, a mutation must not only increase information but also be beneficial, so that natural selection causes it to be incorporated into the population. Of all the possible mutations that can occur, only a tiny fraction will result in an increase in information—but the majority of these will not confer any benefit on the organism. For example, a mutation might occur which produces additional hair growth when the climate is becoming warmer. A mutation might cause an animal to grow a longer neck when the food source is close to the ground. If evolution were true, we would expect to see information-increasing mutations occurring regularly. The fact that they are so rare is strong evidence against the neo-Darwinian theory.

Creation scientists do not claim that it is *impossible* for information-increasing mutations to occur—they could occur, theoretically, and this may well have happened. Rather, they argue that, for significant amounts of useful genetic information to be *built up* in a population, too many rare and unlikely events must take place. Firstly, there is a very small probability of a beneficial, information-increasing mutation occurring, as the vast majority of mutations are detrimental and information-losing.[8] Secondly, even if such a mutation does occur, there is only a small probability of it conferring a benefit that is sufficiently advantageous so as to make it amenable to natural selection.[9] Thirdly, studies of population genetics show that, even if a significantly beneficial mutation does occur, there is only a small probability of it spreading to the rest of the population.[10] Fourthly, many, many of these unlikely events are required to effect significant evolutionary change.

Evolutionists sometimes respond to this kind of argument by saying that, since evolution operates over such long timescales (millions of years), the probabilities are much more plausible than they might first appear. Professor Dawkins, for example, discusses the unlikely event of a perfect deal in bridge, where each of the four players receives thirteen cards of the same suit. Although very improbable, he considers this to be within the 'range of more or less improbable events that do sometimes happen'.[11] Hence, he argues, if we lived for millions of years, we would not regard such events as so unexpected.[12] Similarly, it is often said of evolutionary processes, that, given enough time, 'anything can happen'. This, however, is unrealistic because, if the probability of something happening is really miniscule, even if it is tried again and again over millions of years, it still cannot be expected to happen. This can be illustrated for the case of the perfect deal in bridge. The probability of a perfect deal is less than 1 in two thousand million million million million (actually 0.00000000000000000000000000000447).[13] Suppose we played ten hands every day for a billion years. During this time, we would play 3,650,000,000,000 hands. To obtain an estimate of the probability of a perfect deal occurring at least once, we can use a simple calculation in which we multiply 3,650,000,000,000 by 0.00000000000000000000000000000447. This gives us the minute probability of less than 1 in six hundred million million (actually 0.00000000000000163). Similarly, as we shall see, the availability of millions of years (and millions of organisms on millions of planets) does not address the improbability of evolution theory either.

In order for new traits to evolve, often a number of favourable mutations must occur together. For example, based on studies of fruit flies, the cell biologist Professor E. J. Ambrose of London University argued that it is unlikely that fewer than five genes could ever be involved in the formation of even the simplest new structure. The chance of five favourable mutations occurring in just the right genes, he concluded, is 'effectively zero'.[14] Moreover, at the level of the organism, the evolution of new functions, such as the ability to fly, would require many specific and novel structures to arise together. According to Professor Andrew McIntosh, who worked in aeronautics at the Royal Aircraft Establishment

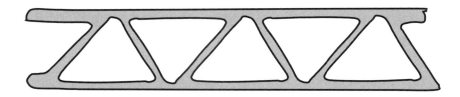

Fig. 20 Truss structure inside a wing bone of a large bird
From Stuart Burgess, *Hallmarks of Design*. Used by permission.

and at the Cranfield Institute of Technology, for a bird to have evolved proficient flight, six characteristics would have had to be developed more or less simultaneously.

Firstly, the bird's bones must be lightweight, which is achieved by their being hollow, sometimes with a truss arrangement of spars inside to give additional load-bearing strength (Fig. 20). Secondly, the wings must be light, but wind resistant. This is achieved through feathers that have a

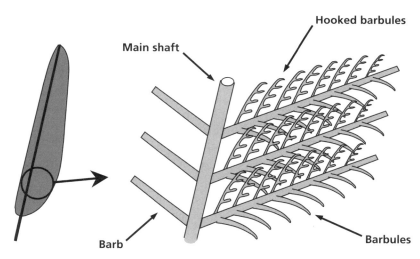

Fig. 21 Simplified diagram of feather structure
From Stuart Burgess, *Hallmarks of Design*

system of barbs and barbules that enable the surface of the feather to be flexible but remain intact (Fig. 21). Unless the barbules have all hooks on one side with all ridged rods on the other, then the feather will not function. Thirdly, this mechanism must be lubricated to prevent it wearing, for which the bird produces oil from a gland at the base of its spine. Fourthly, in order to preen and oil its feathers, the bird must have developed the capacity to rotate its head 180°. Fifthly, the flapping motion of the wings requires two main wing muscles, rather than the one main muscle possessed by most land-based creatures for flexing a limb. Sixthly, these muscles require a high source of energy to operate, so that normal respiration is not good enough. Some small birds, for example, breathe about 250 times per minute. To achieve this, the air is fed straight into air sacs, which are connected directly to the bloodstream, with airflow going in both directions in the lung. As one air sac inflates, another deflates, quite unlike other land-based creatures.

Of all the possible mutations that could occur, only a tiny fraction will produce a new function. Of the tiny fraction of mutations that could produce a new function, only a tiny fraction of these would contribute to the development of flight. The probability of numerous mutations occurring that contribute to the evolution of flight, even gradually over millions of years, is just too small to be considered plausible. As Professor McIntosh concluded, 'Flight alone demolishes any concept of evolution.'[15]

Significantly, some geneticists argue that, rather than mutations providing the potential to improve populations, it is much more likely that they will, over time, destroy them.[16] For example, in his book *Genetic Entropy and the Mystery of the Genome*, Dr Sanford argues that the effect of harmful mutations greatly outweighs any benefit that there might be from the occasional beneficial mutation, and that genomes must therefore inexorably degenerate.[17] Along with many others, he draws attention to the fact that, currently, the number of mutations carried by humans rises every generation. As a conservative estimate, each birth adds around 100 new mutations to the population, of which the vast majority are, of course, deleterious.[18] The consequences of this are not seen in any great measure currently for a number of reasons, one of which is that most of these mutations are 'near-neutral' in their effect. That is, although they are detrimental and therefore harmful, they are only very slightly harmful. Because they have so little effect, they are not removed from the population by natural selection and, in most cases, the carrier is not even aware of them.[19] As a result, the number of mutations in the population continues to grow, virtually unabated. This situation cannot continue indefinitely, however, because there will come a point, many generations hence, when these 'near-neutral' mutations start to combine. According to Dr Sanford, the consequences of this, ultimately, will be lethal:

… there is no selection scheme that can reverse the damage … we are on a downward slide that cannot be stopped. When selection is unable to counter the loss of information due to mutations, a situation arises called 'error catastrophe'. If not rapidly corrected, this situation leads to the eventual death of the species—extinction. In its final stages, genomic degeneration leads to declining fertility, which curtails further selection … Inbreeding and genetic drift must then take over entirely—rapidly finishing off the genome. When this point is reached, the process becomes an irreversible downward spiral … Based on numerous independent lines of evidence, we are forced to conclude that the problem of human genomic degeneration is real. While selection is essential for slowing down degeneration, no form of selection can actually halt it … The extinction of the human genome appears to be just as certain and deterministic as the extinction of stars, the death of organisms, and the heat death of the universe.[20]

Computer simulations, even using data favourable to evolution, have consistently supported this prediction.[21]

Evolutionists sometimes argue that an organism's genetic information can be increased by DNA 'insertions', when mutations result in single or multiple nucleotides (genetic letters) being added. These are, however, powerless to create significant amounts of information and almost always destroy it, as explained by Dr Don Batten:

The information on the DNA is like written language: the sequence of base [nucleotide] pairs, like the letters in written language, codes for something meaningful (often an amino acid sequence for a protein, like insulin or hemoglobin). Take the sentence: 'The cat sat off the mat' (the choice of 3-letter words was deliberate, because it reflects the triplet genetic code, explained below). Now let us insert a letter (like a base [nucleotide] insertion in DNA): 'The ciat sat off the mat.' The sentence now has an extra letter. Does it now have more information? No, it is basically meaningless; it no longer specifies anything meaningful. The insertion has destroyed the information, not added to it. Actually, it's worse than that with DNA, because insertion of a base ('letter') results in all the information downstream from the insertion being garbled. Because each 'word' in the DNA is fixed at three letters, it would now read as the completely nonsensical: 'The cia tsa tof fth ema t.' Deletions have a similar effect of creating garbage downstream from the deletion.[22]

Another way evolutionists argue that genetic information could be built up is through 'gene duplication'. This is where an organism accidentally makes an extra copy of a gene (or part of a gene or a number of genes), which, indeed, can and does happen. However, a copy of a gene is not new information—it is just a copy of existing information. To create new information, the copied DNA must mutate so that it has a different and useful function. The gene duplication idea holds that the copied gene can lie dormant ('unexpressed') so that it is free to mutate without this affecting the organism. Occasionally, by chance, such a gene could mutate into something favourable. Then, again by chance, this new gene could somehow become activated ('expressed') and give rise to some new function.

The problems with this theory, however, are enormous. In particular, the 'sequence space' (the number of possible 'genetic letter' arrangements) in just one gene is so large that the chance of finding anything useful by making random changes is indescribably small.[23] Just as the likelihood of producing a new, meaningful paragraph in English by randomly selecting letters and spaces is negligible, so is the chance of finding a new, functional gene by randomly selecting from 'genetic letters'. As explained by Professor Paul Davies of Arizona State University, 'Only a very tiny fraction of all possible sequences spells out a biologically meaningful message … Another way of expressing this is to say that genes and proteins require exceedingly high degrees of specificity in their structure.'[24] Moreover, to facilitate evolutionary progression, it is not sufficient to find just any new sequence which is, theoretically, biologically functional—

particular sequences must be found which will be useful to the organism at each stage of its evolutionary development. In some cases, a whole system of very specific new genes might be needed. The idea that these new genes could have been found by random searches is highly questionable, as illustrated by Dr Sarfati:

There could never be enough 'experiments' (mutating generations of organisms) to find anything useful by such a process. Note that an average gene of 1,000 base pairs [genetic letters] represents $4^{1,000}$ possibilities—that is 10^{602} (compare this with the number of atoms in the universe estimated at 'only' 10^{80}).[25] If every atom in the universe represented an 'experiment' every millisecond for the supposed 15 billion years of the universe, this could only try a maximum 10^{100} of the possibilities for the gene.[26]

According to this scenario, which is ridiculously favourable to evolution, the fraction of the total number of possibilities that could be tried is, i.e.

$$\frac{10^{100}}{10^{602}} = \frac{1}{10^{502}} \text{ i.e. } \frac{1}{1 \text{ followed by 502 zeroes}}$$

This is unimaginably small.

The argument that the new sequences could have been found through a neo-Darwinian 'step-by-step' process seems to fare little better. This is because, generally, useful sequences appear to be not just very *rare*, but also *isolated* from one another.[27] In such cases, the mutated 'transitional sequences' would not only function less well than the sequences from which they are derived, but would probably stop working altogether before reaching a new, useful form. In some cases, the transitional sequences would actually be harmful. The isolated nature of many functional sequences is shown in Fig. 22. Here an optimized sequence is represented as the top of a hill. To move from one optimized sequence to another, it is necessary to move down the slope of one hill (becoming less optimized), before climbing the slope of another. Rather than facilitating such a process, natural selection would tend to keep the gene at the top of the hill—that is, it would tend to preserve the optimum sequence.

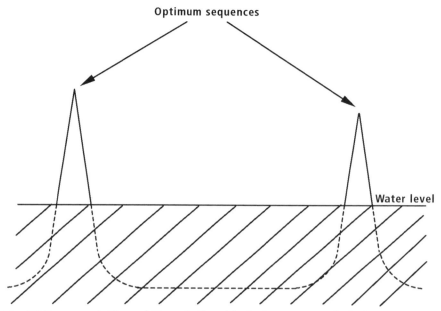

Fig. 22 Representation of the relationship between genetic letter sequence and function

The horizontal dimension represents sequence space, and hill height represents proficiency in performing a biological function. The water level indicates the minimum level of function that could be biologically useful. Sequences around the bottom of the trough may even be harmful.

The probability of genomes having been built through random mutations is actually even lower than the above illustrations would suggest. This is because at least some DNA sequences are 'polyfunctional', meaning they are read in more than one way.[28] A helpful analogy here is, again, a written sentence. In English, a sentence is read once, from left to right. A 'polyfunctional' sentence might be read from left to right to obtain one instruction, and then from right to left to obtain another. A third instruction might be obtained by reading every other letter. In a written language like English, it is theoretically possible for random typing errors to increase the amount of information in a sentence—by adding a few letters or words, for example. However, where DNA sequences are polyfunctional, it is almost impossible for information to be increased through a copying error; even if a mutation caused a sequence to contain more information when read in one way, it would almost always have corrupted the information that is read in the other ways.[29]

The probability of all that we see in the living world evolving by random processes is so small that it is difficult to describe. The late world-renowned physicist/astronomer Professor Fred Hoyle estimated the probability of *just one* of the many proteins or DNA molecules upon which life depends forming by the random shuffling of chemicals in a 'primordial soup'. This, he found, is about the same as the probability of 10^{50} blind people (that is, 1 followed by fifty zeros), each with a scrambled Rubik's Cube, simultaneously arriving at the solved form. Such an idea, he concluded, is 'evidently nonsense of a high order'.[30] Speaking of the idea that random genetic mutations could give rise to the evolution of the eye, Pierre-Paul Grassé, arguably France's most distinguished zoologist, commented, 'There is no law against day-dreaming, but science must not indulge in it.'[31] The biologist and Nobel Prizewinner Jacques Monod suggested that the probability of life emerging from inanimate matter is so small that it might be considered to be 'zero'.[32]

The most common response by evolutionists to the claim that theory of evolution is too improbable to be believed is that the process does not rely on purely random events. They argue that, because the path is guided by natural selection, which 'chooses between the good and bad mutations', the improbable becomes probable, or even inevitable. This, however, does not fit the facts.

Firstly, in respect of chemical evolution, which supposedly explains how the first protein and DNA molecules were formed, natural selection is inoperative. This is because 'growing' proteins and DNA molecules are not self-reproducing.[33] As explained by the late Theodosius Dobzhansky, who was Professor of Zoology at Columbia University and Professor of Genetics at the University of California, 'In order to have natural selection, you have to have self-reproduction ... Prebiological natural selection is a contradiction of terms.'[34] Similarly, Professor Davies argues, '... Darwinian evolution can operate only if life of some sort already exists (strictly, it requires not life in its full glory, only replication, variation and selection). Darwinism can offer no help at all in explaining that all-important first step: the origin of life.'[35]

Secondly, natural selection is unable to act on the vast majority of mutations (whether good or bad) because they have too small an effect. As an illustration, Dr Sanford asks us to consider the effect of one soldier in a very large army, where the army is analogous to an organism and the replacing of a solider analogous to a mutation. In most cases, if one soldier is replaced by a much better or a much worse soldier, the difference in performance of the whole army would be negligible.[36]

Thirdly, natural selection can never create anything—all it can do is 'choose' between different 'variants' which are already there. The point is made clearly by Gerd Müller, Professor of Zoology at the University of Vienna: '… selection has no innovative capacity: it eliminates or maintains what exists.'[37] And, as we have seen, it is highly questionable as to whether random mutations can produce viable variants from which natural selection can choose, even over millions of years.

Fourthly, it should be realized that natural selection, if it is to direct significant evolutionary change, requires that a sequence of small steps actually exists by which an organism can change from one form to another. The Nobel Prizewinner Professor Brian Josephson remarks,

… a crucial part of the argument concerns whether there exists a continuous path, leading from the origins of life to man, each step of which is both favoured by natural selection, and small enough to have happened by chance. It appears to be presented [by some evolutionists] as a matter of logical necessity that such a path exists, but actually there is no such logical necessity …[38]

Fifthly, in practice, when natural selection does act, it is often seen to reduce genetic information, not increase it, which is the opposite of what is required for 'molecules-to-man' evolution. As explained by the geneticist Professor Maciej Giertych, 'adapted populations are genetically poorer (fewer alleles[39]) than the unselected natural populations from which they arose.'[40] This is not difficult to understand and, as an illustration, we may turn to the classic textbook example of the 'evolution of the peppered

Fig. 23 Light and dark peppered moths against a dark tree trunk. Photograph by Michael W. Tweedie, Science Photo Library.

moth' (*Biston betularia*). Peppered moths are found in both light and dark colours. In England, prior to the nineteenth century, the lighter-coloured moths were very common and the darker-coloured moths very rare. However, towards the end of the nineteenth century, darker-coloured moths were found in abundance. The usual explanation for this is that pollution generated by the burning of coal during the Industrial Revolution darkened the bark of trees,[41] resulting in lighter-coloured moths becoming more conspicuous when they settled on tree trunks and being picked off and eaten by birds (Fig. 23). Consequently, the darker-coloured moths were naturally selected and became more abundant. Had the pollution continued and become more widespread, the lighter moths would have probably become extinct. However, assuming that all this is substantially correct, how does it relate to genetic information? The answer is that it would *deplete* the gene pool (resulting in a loss of information), as the new population would no longer include moths that carry the gene which produces lighter-coloured offspring. In this respect, natural selection is similar to selective breeding. When dogs, for example, are selectively bred to produce a new special breed, so much genetic information is lost that it is impossible to selectively breed the new dogs so as to reproduce the characteristics of the original dogs.

Although rarely publicized, serious problems with Neo-Darwinian Theory have been known for many years. In 1970, the biochemist and Nobel Prizewinner Professor Ernst Chain FRS said of this that it is a 'hypothesis based on no evidence and irreconcilable with the facts'.[42] Speaking of the idea that genes that specify functional proteins could have arisen through accident or by trial and error, he commented, 'The probability for such an event to have occurred is just too small to be seriously considered.'[43] In 1982, Professors Hoyle and Wickramasinghe produced what they described as a 'simple and decisive disproof of the [neo-]Darwinian theory'.[44] More recently, the neo-Darwinian theory has been challenged by a host of scientific essays and books.[45] Although accepting (along with many creationists) the role of variation and natural selection in micro-evolutionary change, many evolutionists doubt the power of the neo-Darwinian theory to explain how macro-evolutionary change could occur. Professor Scott Gilbert comments,

… starting in the 1970s, many biologists began questioning its adequacy in explaining evolution. Genetics might be adequate for explaining microevolution, but microevolutionary changes in gene frequency were not seen as able to turn a reptile into a mammal or to convert a fish into an amphibian. Microevolution looks at adaptations that concern the survival of the fittest, not the arrival of the fittest. As Goodwin points out, 'the origins of species—Darwin's problem remains unsolved'.[46]

Professor Stuart Kauffman, leader of the Institute for Biocomplexity and Informatics at the University of Calgary, Canada, also argues that random mutations and natural selection are inadequate to explain the evolution of complex organisms. Instead, he suggests that there must be self-organizing mechanisms in nature that facilitate the neo-Darwinian process. He freely admits, however, 'We have no such framework as yet.'[47]

According to the information scientist Werner Gitt, who was a Professor and Director at the Federal Institute of Physics and Technology, Braunschweig, Germany, 'There is no known law of nature, no known process and no sequence of events which can cause information to originate by itself in matter.'[48] Moreover, not only are the information-generating processes that are required for 'molecules-to-man' evolution not observed in nature, some leading mathematicians have even speculated that, one day, there may be a formal proof that they will never be found.[49]

What, then, is the explanation for the observed processes of speciation? The clue to answering this question probably lies in the little-known fact that these processes can be very fast. Having studied the rate of speciation of finches on the Galápagos Islands, Professor Peter Grant of Princeton University concluded that the medium ground finch could become a large ground finch in as little as 200 years.[50] In another study of island finches, significant changes in beak shape were observed in only twenty years.[51] It is wholly untenable to argue that such rapid speciation occurs through random genetic mutation and natural selection because such a process (if it worked at all) would require many thousands of years.[52] It is far more likely that these changes arise from the sorting of or selection from an *existing* rich and varied gene pool, through normal, everyday variation coupled with natural selection, and/or the triggering of pre-programmed genetic options by the environment.

The ability of organisms to change in response to changes in their environment has been widely observed in both plants and animals for many years and is known as *phenotypic plasticity*.[53] The changes can take place very rapidly (sometimes in no more than a generation) and have been observed to be both heritable and reversible. There are many examples of phenotypic plasticity. Plants adjust their seed production according to how densely they populate an area, producing fewer seeds if their cover is dense and more seeds if their cover is sparse; the rate at which fish grow to reproductive maturity can be influenced by the kinds of predators they face, maturing faster if the predators favour small, immature fish and slower if they favour large, mature fish; the jaw bones and jaw muscles of rodents have been seen to change significantly through changes in diet; the temperature at which fish are raised can determine the number of vertebrae they grow; the shells of snails can become thicker when a predator is introduced. In some cases, the changes are so significant that two genetically identical organisms can be mistaken for two different species.[54] In fewer than forty years, lizards have been known to exhibit not only significant changes in bite force, head size and head shape, but also dramatic changes in gut morphology. This has even included the appearance of a new valve, used to slow down the passage of food.[55] In all these cases, the speed of change is far too fast for it to arise through mutations and natural selection. Such examples of adaptation cannot, therefore, be used to illustrate 'molecules-to-man' evolution because all the evidence indicates that it is *existing* genetic information that effects the change. Neither is there any evidence that such processes can lead to one kind of animal turning into another kind of animal—as far as we know, birds always remain birds, fish always remain fish, and so on.

Similar processes could explain how the many species observed on the earth today could have arisen from the limited number of animals that disembarked from Noah's ark.[56] According to this model, as these creatures reproduced and their offspring gradually spread out away from the ark's final resting place, the original gene pools, capable of producing all manner of species, were distributed over the earth. Hence, for example, all the species of the dog kind seen today (wolf, dingo, jackal, fox, etc.) could have arisen from just one pair of dogs; all the species of the horse kind (zebra, donkey, Shetland pony, etc.) could have arisen from one pair of horses. This could have occurred as a result of geographical isolation coupled with natural selection in a similar way to that in which new species can be produced artificially through selective breeding. Animals that are specially adapted to their environments, such as polar bears, might have developed characteristics such as extra heat insulation by cold conditions triggering the use of genes that produce a thicker layer of blubber.[57] Moreover, many diverse animals could have arisen from each original kind simply because they were created with the genetic information capable of producing significant variation.

Notes

1 The human genome, for example, has around three billion genetic letters.
2 **Paul Davies,** *The Fifth Miracle* (London: Penguin, 1999); **Werner Gitt,** *In the Beginning Was Information* (Bielefeld: Christliche Literatur-Verbreitung, 1997), p. 107.
3 **Kevin L. Anderson** and **Georgia Purdom,** 'A Creationist Perspective of Beneficial Mutations in Bacteria', *Proceedings of the Sixth International Conference on Creationism* (Creation Science Fellowship, 2008), pp. 73–86.
4 **Lee Spetner,** *Not by Chance* (New York: Judaica Press, 1998), p. 143.
5 Ibid. p. 169. See also pp. 138 and 159–160.
6 Lee Spetner/Edward Max dialogue, 2001, at: trueorigin.org.
7 **John Sanford,** *Genetic Entropy and the Mystery of the Genome* (New York: Ivan Press, 2005), p. 17.
8 Ibid. ch. 2.
9 Ibid. ch. 4.
10 **Ronald A. Fisher,** *The Genetical Theory of Natural Selection* (Oxford: Oxford University Press, 1999), ch. 4, pp. 76–77.
11 **Richard Dawkins,** *The Blind Watchmaker* (London: Penguin, 1986), p. 161.
12 Ibid. p. 162.
13 **N. T. Gridgeman,** 'The Mystery of the Missing Deal', *The American Statistician*, 1/8 (1964), pp. 15–16.
14 **Edmund J. Ambrose,** *The Nature and Origin of the Biological World* (Chichester: Ellis Horwood, 1982), p. 120.
15 **Andy McIntosh,** *Genesis for Today* (3rd edn.; Leominster: Day One, 2006), pp. 194–196.
16 **Jerry Bergman,** 'Progressive Evolution or Degeneration?', *Proceedings of the Sixth International Conference on Creationism*, pp. 99–110.
17 **Sanford,** *Genetic Entropy and the Mystery of the Genome.*
18 Ibid. ch. 3.
19 Ibid. ch. 4.
20 Ibid. pp. 40–41, 83.
21 **John Baumgardner et al.,** 'Mendel's Accountant: A New Population Genetics Simulation Tool for Studying Mutation and Natural Selection', *Proceedings of the Sixth International Conference on Creationism*, pp. 87–98; John Baumgardner et al., 'Using Numerical Simulation to Test the Validity of Neo-Darwinian Theory', *Proceedings of the Sixth*

International Conference on Creationism, pp. 165–175. Clearly, the Bible predicts Christ's return before the extinction of the human race!

22 **Don Batten,** CMI and Spetner Questioned on Soundness of Science', Feedback, *Creation*, 7 March 2005, at: creationontheweb.com; answersingenesis.org.

23 **Royal Truman** and **Peter Borger,** 'Genome Truncation vs Mutational Opportunity: Can New Genes Arise via Gene Duplication? Part 1', *TJ* (Journal of Creation) 22/1, p. 108.

24 **Davies,** *The Fifth Miracle*, p. 92.

25 There are four different genetic letters (that is, bases or nucleotides): A, T, C and G. The number of ways in which these four letters can be arranged in a 1,000-letter sequence is $4^{1,000}$. Note that $4^{1,000}$ is 4 multiplied by itself 999 times; 10^{602} is 1 followed by 602 zeros; 10^{80} is 1 followed by 80 zeros.

26 **Jonathan Sarfati,** *Refuting Evolution 2* (Green Forest, AR: Master Books, 2002), p. 107; see creationontheweb.com/content/view/3268.

27 **Stephen C. Meyer,** 'The Origin of Biological Information and the Higher Taxonomic Categories', *Proceedings of the Biological Society of Washington*, 117/2 (2004), pp. 213–239, at: discovery.org.

28 This may not apply to the genomes of prokaryotes (e.g. bacteria).

29 There are many ways in which DNA is polyfunctional. Intron/exon splicing gives multiple varieties of mRNA per gene. Around 25,000 genes can produce as many as 100,000 to 300,000 proteins. DNA can simultaneously code for genes and histone binding sites. One gene can have an effect on many parts of the body. Perhaps the most remarkable way in which DNA is polyfunctional (and therefore also polyconstrained) is that, sometimes, both the sense and antisense strands are transcribed. DNA appears also to be read three-dimensionally. **Sanford,** *Genetic Entropy and the Mystery of the Genome*, pp. 131–133; **Alex Williams,** 'Astonishing DNA Complexity Demolishes Neo-Darwinism', *TJ* (Journal of Creation) 21/3, pp. 111–117.

30 **Fred Hoyle,** 'The Big Bang in Astronomy', *New Scientist*, 19 November 1981, p. 527.

31 **Pierre Grassé,** *Evolution of Living Organisms* (New York: Academic Press, 1977), p. 104.

32 Cited by **Karl R. Popper,** 'Scientific Reduction and the Essential Incompleteness of all Science', in **F. J. Ayala,** and **T. Dobzhansky,** (eds.), *Studies in the Philosophy of Biology* (London: Macmillan, 1974), p. 270.

33 Furthermore, proteins and nucleic acids, which are very long and complex molecules, would tend to break down in a 'primordial ocean', rather than gradually build themselves up over thousands or millions of years. See **Lawrence R. Croft,** *How Life Began* (Darlington: Evangelical Press, 1988), p. 155.

34 Theodosius Dobzhansky, cited by **George Schramm** in **S. W. Fox,** (ed.), 'The Origins of Prebiological Systems and of their Molecular Matrices', *Proceedings of a Conference Conducted at Wakulla Springs, Florida, 27–30 October 1963* (New York: Academic Press, 1965), pp. 309–315.

35 Davies, *The Fifth Miracle*, p. 20.

36 Sanford, *Genetic Entropy and the Mystery of the Genome*, p. 49.

37 Gerd Müller, 'Homology: The Evolution of Morphological Organization', in **Gerd Müller** and **Stuart Newman,** (eds.), *Origination of Organismal Form: Beyond the Gene in Developmental and Evolutionary Biology* (Cambridge, MA: MIT Press, 2003), p. 51.

38 Brian Josephson, 'Science Giants Do a Good Job: We're Hooked and Keen to Learn', Letters, *The Independent on Sunday*, 12 January 1997.

39 An allele is one of two or more alternative forms of a gene that determines the same characteristic but produces a different effect. For example, the eye-colour gene can have a 'brown' or 'blue' allele.

40 Maciej Giertych, 'Professor of Genetics Says "No!" to Evolution', *Creation*, 17/3 (1995), pp. 46–48, at: creationontheweb.com; answersingenesis.org.

41 That is, it is understood that pollution killed the light-coloured lichens that covered the trees, thus exposing the dark bark.

42 Ernst Chain, *Social Responsibility and the Scientist in Modern Western Society* (London: The Council of Christians and Jews, 1970), p. 25.

43 Ibid. p. 26.

44 Fred Hoyle and **Chandra Wickramasinghe,** *Why Neo-Darwinism Does Not Work* (Cardiff: University College Cardiff Press, 1982).

45 Meyer, 'The Origin of Biological Information and the Higher Taxonomic Categories'.

46 Scott Gilbert et al., 'Resynthesizing Evolutionary and Developmental Biology', *Developmental Biology*, 173 (1996), pp. 357–372.

47 Stuart Kauffman, *At Home in the Universe. The Search for Laws of Self-Organisation and Complexity* (New York: Oxford University Press, 1995), p. 150.

48 Gitt, *In the Beginning Was Information*, p. 107.

49 John Lennox, *God's Undertaker* (Oxford: Lion Hudson, 2007), ch. 9.

50 Peter Grant, 'Natural Selection and Darwin's Finches', *Scientific American*, 265/4 (1991), pp. 60–65.

51 Sheila Conant, 'Saving Endangered Species by Translocation', *BioScience*, 38/4 (1988), 254–257; **Stuart Pimm,** 'Rapid Morphological Change in an Introduced Bird', *Trends in Evolution and Ecology*, 3/11 (1988), pp. 290–291.

52 **Todd C. Wood,** *A Creationist Review and Preliminary Analysis of the History, Geology, Climate and Biology of the Galápagos Islands* (Eugene, OR: Wipf and Stock, 2005), p. 122.

53 **Spetner,** *Not by Chance*, ch. 7.

54 **Anurag A. Agrawal,** 'Phenotypic Plasticity in the Interactions and Evolution of Species', *Science*, 294 (2001), pp. 321–326.

55 **Anthony Herrel et al.,** 'Rapid Large-Scale Evolutionary Divergence in Morphology and Performance Associated with Exploitation of a Different Dietary Resource', *Proceedings of the National Academy of Sciences USA*, 105/12, pp. 4792–4795.

56 **Jean Lightner,** 'Life: Designed by God to Adapt', 4 June, 2008, at: answersingenesis.org.

57 **David Tyler,** 'Polar Bears … One of a (Created) Kind', *Origins*, 44 (2006), pp. 8–11, at: biblicalcreation.org.uk.

Homology

Evolutionists argue that 'homologies' of common anatomy and common DNA, shared by many different organisms, offer strong evidence that the various plants and animals observed today evolved from common ancestors. For example, many animals have four limbs, two eyes and two ears, supposedly indicating descent from a common evolutionary ancestor having these characteristics. Indeed, the apparent relationships between some homologous structures are striking, as can be seen in Fig. 24. There are many similarities between the DNA of humans and that of chimpanzees (and other animals), again supposedly indicating that both evolved from a common ancestor with similar DNA. The genetic code itself is almost universal across organisms. There is, however, an alternative explanation for these similarities—a common designer.

One of the strongest arguments in support of homologies being evidence of a common designer, rather than a common evolutionary ancestor, is found in the study of embryos. For example, the digits (fingers and thumbs) of humans form by the material of the hand dissolving between them,[1] whereas in frogs these grow outwardly from buds (Fig. 25).[2] If frogs and humans both have digits because they evolved from a common ancestor with digits, as evolutionists believe, one would expect their embryonic development to be similar. In his book *Homology, an Unsolved Problem*, Sir Gavin de Beer FRS, who was Professor of Embryology at the University of London, gives some excellent examples of how the embryonic development of the same structures in fish, amphibia, reptiles and mammals can be markedly different. Consider, for example, the alimentary canal (the passage along which food passes from the mouth to the anus during digestion). In sharks, this is formed from the roof of the embryonic gut; in the lamprey, from the floor; in frogs, from the roof and floor; and in birds and reptiles, from the embryonic disc (blastoderm).[3] The classic example of homology—the vertebrate forelimbs—again fails when subjected to closer scrutiny (Fig. 26). Not only do they develop quite differently, but they also grow from different parts of the embryo: in the newt (an amphibian), they develop from the trunk segments 2 to 5; in the

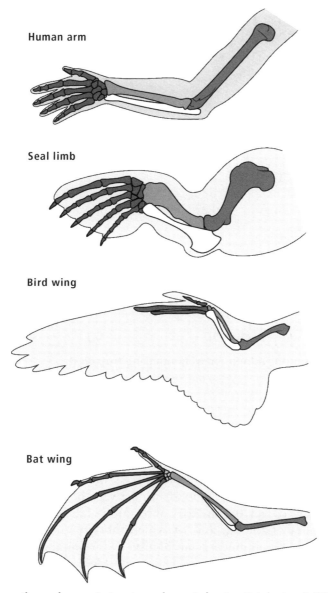

Human arm

Seal limb

Bird wing

Bat wing

Fig. 24 Some 'homologous' structures in vertebrates © John Lewis 2009

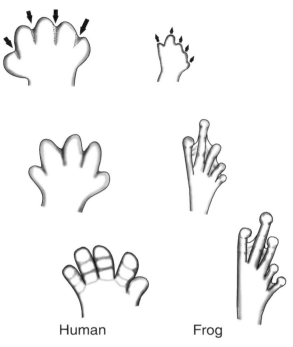

Fig. 25 Embryonic development of human and frog digits
From *Creation*, creationontheweb.com. Used by permission.

lizard (a reptile), from segments 6 to 9; and in man (a mammal), from segments 13 to 18.[4] Faced with many such examples, Professor de Beer concluded, 'It does not seem to matter where in the egg or the embryo the living substance out of which homologous organs are formed comes from.'[5] 'The fact is that correspondence between homologous structures cannot be pressed back to similarity of position of the cells in the embryo, or of the parts of the egg out of which the structures are ultimately composed, or of developmental mechanism by which they are formed.'[6]

According to the late Harvard University biologist Dr Pere Alberch, such differences in the development of homologous structures are 'the rule rather than the exception'.[7]

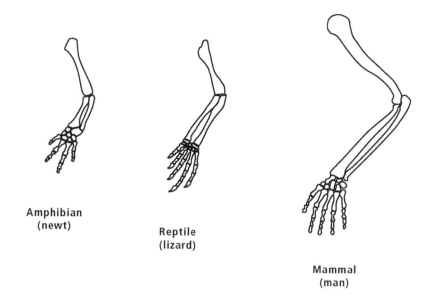

Fig. 26 Vertebrate forelimbs

These are considered to be strictly homologous, but they develop differently and from different parts of the embryo.

Arguably, an even greater problem for evolutionary theory arose when it was discovered that homologous structures in different animal kinds are often specified by different genes. As Professor de Beer put it,

Because homology implies community of descent from ... a common ancestor it might be thought that genetics would provide the key to the problem of homology. This is where the worst shock of all is encountered ... [because] homologous structures need not be controlled by identical genes ... It is now clear that the pride with which it was assumed that the inheritance of homologous structures from a common ancestor explained homology was misplaced; for such inheritance cannot be ascribed to identity of genes. The attempt to find 'homologous' genes, except in closely related species, has been given up as hopeless.[8]

Indeed, as explained by Rolf Sattler, Professor of Biology at McGill University, '… in general the homology of structures such as organs or modules cannot be ascribed to inheritance of homologous genes or sets of genes. Consequently, organ homology cannot be reduced to gene homology.'[9]

Similarly, Gunter Wagner, Professor of Ecology and Evolutionary Biology at Yale University, laments that 'The disturbingly many and deep problems associated with any attempt to identify the biological basis of homology have been presented repeatedly … it is important to note the common theme in complaints of the inadequacy of developmental biology and genetics to account for homology.'[10]

Given that genetic inheritance is the foundation of evolutionary theory, can it really be argued that homologous structures indicate common evolutionary ancestry when the genes that produce them are different?

Moreover, not only is the development of homologous structures often controlled by different genes, but the development of non-homologous structures is often found to be controlled by the same genes. For example, the gene *Distal-less* is known to be involved in the development of various appendages in organisms as diverse as mice, worms, butterflies and sea urchins.[11] Again, the association between the same genes and several non-homologous structures seems to be the rule rather than the exception.[12] Significantly, the discovery that the development of homologous structures is often controlled by different genes was to Professor de Beer 'a shock', and the discovery that the development of non-homologous structures is often controlled by the same genes was to Professor Gould 'explicitly unexpected'.[13] Clearly, these evolutionists would not have predicted these findings.

When a more than cursory examination of nature is undertaken, it is clear that it is essentially *discontinuous*. Amphibia supposedly evolved into reptiles, but the egg of the reptile is vastly more complex and, in many ways, essentially different from that of an amphibian. In fact, there are hardly two eggs in the whole animal kingdom that differ more fundamentally. Reptiles supposedly evolved into birds, but the lungs of reptiles are of a bellows configuration, with the air reversing direction as the animal breathes in and out, whereas the lungs of birds are a straight-through design, a system enhanced by birds having hollow bones. The scales of reptiles, which are basically thickened skin, cannot be compared with feathers, which are the most complex and intricate of structures, made up of millions of components. Reptiles supposedly also evolved into mammals, but comparisons of their respective hearts and blood vessels do not support this. In reptiles, the aorta (the artery which carries the oxygenated blood away from the heart) is formed from a blood vessel coming from the right, whereas in mammals, it comes from the left.[14] The platypus is another creature that presents a major problem for evolutionary theory. This is because it incorporates features of mammals, birds and reptiles. For example, it has fur and produces milk for its young like a mammal, has webbed feet and a beak like a bird, and produces venom and lays eggs like a reptile. Consequently, it is difficult to argue that it can be either the ancestor or the descendant of any of these three classes of vertebrates.[15] Rather than being an example of evolution, the platypus appears to have been created with a mosaic of features normally characteristic of different animals.

If evolution between the basic animal kinds had occurred, we would expect to observe the same fundamental pattern of *continuity* seen when speciation within a kind occurs. For example, there is a clear continuum between the herring gull (*Larus argentatus*) and the lesser black-backed gull (*Larus fuscus*). Although in Europe they are two distinct species that do not naturally interbreed, it is possible to see the progression from one to the other simply by travelling further and further east from Russia. Evolutionists contend that the transitional forms between the basic animal kinds are not seen today because they have died out. But is it really credible that *all* of them have died out?

Evolutionists argue that the difference between the genomes of humans and chimpanzees is 'only' around 4 or 5 per cent, indicating that we are very closely related.[16] However, due to these genomes being so large, this actually amounts to an enormous difference in genetic information. In fact, there are around 35 million 'genetic letters' that are different, plus around 45 million found in the human that are absent from the chimp and around 45 million found in the chimp that are absent from the human.[17] Moreover, humans and chimpanzees are now known to have different amino-acid sequences in a least 55 per cent of their proteins.[18] According to Professor David DeWitt, around 40 million mutation events would have been required to separate the two species and give rise to such a large difference in their genomes—20 million in the line leading to modern apes, and 20 million in the line leading to modern humans.[19] Evolutionists believe that many of these mutations would have been largely neutral in their effect and therefore not subject to natural selection. But could natural selection have acted on the beneficial mutations so as to change ape-like creatures into humans?

According to evolution theory, ape-like creatures evolved into humans over the last five million years. During this period, many changes and improvements would have had to arise: the tripling of brain size, the evolution of upright posture, hand dexterity, speech organs, language, and the appreciation of music—and much more. But such a high rate of evolution is fraught with difficulties, one of the most problematic being known as 'Haldane's Dilemma'.[20] According to the late Professor J. B. S. Haldane FRS, organisms having reproduction rates similar to those of apes and humans could not incorporate new beneficial mutations into a population faster than one every 300 generations.[21] For an evolving ape/human population, with twenty years per generation, this would limit the number of beneficial mutations that could be accrued in ten million years (twice the available time) to

$$\frac{10,000,000}{300 \times 20} = 1,667$$

This, surely, cannot account for all the changes that would be needed to turn an ape into a human.

The reasoning behind 'Haldane's Dilemma' is not difficult to understand, although it has been greatly confused in the literature. Simply put, evolution requires an extra reproduction rate, which limits the speed at which the changes can occur. Just to maintain its current size, a population must reproduce at a rate much greater than one for one. This is because many offspring will die before they reach reproductive maturity. If a small, evolving population is to *grow* in size (and become the new, predominant species), its members must reproduce even faster. Those who study population genetics sometimes refer to these reproductive requirements as 'costs'. For example, there is a 'cost of random loss', which is the extra reproduction rate required to compensate for losses to the population arising from events such as fire, flood or famine. There is the 'cost of mutation', which is the extra reproduction rate required to compensate for deaths due to harmful mutations. Of particular significance is the 'cost of substitution', which is the extra reproduction rate required to increase the number of organisms carrying the new, beneficial mutations—these mutations begin as one copy, and must then grow in number until a new population arises that has them.[22] The sum of all the 'costs' is the 'cost of evolution', which is the total reproduction rate required of the species in order to make the evolutionary scenario seem plausible. If the reproduction rate of an organism is slow, its evolution can only proceed very slowly.[23] 'Haldane's Dilemma' is a serious problem for evolutionary theory and it has not been solved.[24]

The natural world is undoubtedly ordered, and contains many patterns. The claim of evolutionists, however, that homologies arose through descent from common ancestors, is inconsistent with much of the data. It cannot, therefore, be considered to be a scientific conclusion. Instead, the existence of similar structures in different animal kinds, arising from different developmental pathways controlled by different genes, points to the work of an ingenious and imaginative Creator.

A creationist interpretation of homology

The question as to why God chose such a pattern for the natural world has been a difficult one for creationists. In his book *The Biotic Message,* Walter ReMine argues that similar structures arising from different developmental pathways is a deliberate ploy of the Creator to point away from evolution as an explanation of the natural world. The pattern (of homologies) then points to a designer while frustrating evolutionary explanations for the similarities. Another possible explanation is that God intended man to interact with and relate to the natural word, which he could better understand if he had a similar form. But why should humans be so different from the animals spiritually and yet so close anatomically and genetically? One possible answer may found in God's

---

statement to Adam and Eve after they sinned: 'For dust you are and to dust you will return' (Genesis 3:19). It was only their being made in the image of God and having righteousness that gave them a place above the rest of creation. Without this, they, along with the animals, had no more value than dust. The explanation for homologies, then, may well be theological rather than scientific.

Notes

1 **T. W. Sadler,** *Langman's Medical Embryology* (7th edn.; Baltimore, MD: Williams & Wilkins, 1995), p. 157.

2 **Michael J. Tyler,** *Australian Frogs: A Natural History* (New York: Cornell University Press, 1998), p. 80.

3 **Gavin de Beer,** *Homology, An Unsolved Problem* (Oxford: Oxford University Press, 1971), p. 13.

4 **Paul Nelson** and **Jonathan Wells,** 'Homology in Biology: Problem for Naturalistic Science and Prospect for Intelligent Design', in **John A. Campbell** and **Stephen C. Meyer,** *Darwinism, Design, and Public Education* (East Lancing, MI: Michigan State University Press, 2003), p. 311; **de Beer,** *Homology, An Unsolved Problem*, p. 8.

5 **de Beer,** *Homology, An Unsolved Problem*, p. 13.

6 **Gavin de Beer,** *Embryos and Ancestors* (3rd edn.; London: Oxford University Press, 1958), p. 152.

7 **Pere Alberch,** 'Problems with the Interpretation of Developmental Sequences', *Systematic Zoology*, 34/1 (1985), p. 51.

8 **de Beer,** *Homology, An Unsolved Problem*, pp. 15–16.

9 **Rolf Sattler,** 'Homology: A Continuing Challenge', *Systematic Botany*, 9/4 (1984), p. 386.

10 **Gunter Wagner,** 'The Origin of Morphological Characters and the Biological Basis of Homology', *Evolution*, 43/6 (1989), p. 1163.

11 Since these appendages do not have similar structures and are not believed to have been possessed by a common evolutionary ancestor, evolutionists would not consider them to be homologous.

12 **Jonathan Wells,** *Icons of Evolution* (Washington DC: Regnery Publishing, 2000), pp. 74–76.

13 **Sean B. Carroll,** *Endless Forms Most Beautiful* (London: Phoenix, 2007), p. 72.

14 That is, in reptiles, the aorta is derived from the fourth right aortic arch, whereas in mammals, it is derived from the fourth left aortic arch.

15 **Paula Weston,** 'The Platypus: Still More Questions than Answers for Evolutionists', *Creation*,

24/2 (2002), pp. 40–43, at: creationontheweb.com; **Robert Carter,** 'Platypus Thumbs its Nose (or Bill) at Evolutionary Scientists', 23 May 2008, at: creationontheweb.com.

16 The original estimate of 1 per cent is now known to be wrong, but it is still often quoted (**Jon Cohen,** 'Relative Differences: The Myth of 1%', *Science*, 316/5833 (2007), p. 1836).

17 David A. DeWitt, 'Chimp Genome Sequence Very Different From Man', 5 September 2005, at: creationontheweb.com; answersingenesis.org.

18 Jerry A. Coyne, 'Switching on Evolution: How Does Evo-Devo Explain the Huge Diversity of Life on Earth?', *Nature*, 435 (2005), pp. 1029–1030.

19 DeWitt, 'Chimp Genome Sequence Very Different From Man'.

20 'Haldane's Dilemma', at: creationwiki.org.

21 J. B. S. Haldane, 'The Cost of Natural Selection', *Journal of Genetics*, 55 (1957), pp. 511–524, at: blackwellpublishing.com/ridley/classictexts/haldane2.pdf. In fact, numerical simulations using Mendel's Accountant (at: mendelsaccount.sourceforge.net) have shown Haldane's prediction to be optimistic. The number of mutations that could be substituted is actually lower than this, as reported by John Baumgardner at the International Creation Conference, Pittsburgh, USA, 2008. Walter J. ReMine, *The Biotic Message* (St Paul, MN: St Paul Science, 1993), chs. 8 and 9; **Walter ReMine,** 'Haldane's Dilemma', at: saintpaulscience.com/Haldane.htm.

22 The cost of substitution is sometimes defined as the extra reproduction rate required to replenish (or 'substitute' for) the members that must die out. This, however, can be confusing and leads to a more difficult analysis.

23 Walter J. ReMine, 'Cost Theory and the Cost of Substitution: A Clarification', *TJ* (Journal of Creation), 19/1 (2005), pp. 113–125, at: creationontheweb.com.

24 Don Batten, 'Haldane's Dilemma Has Not Been Solved', *TJ* (Journal of Creation), 19/1 (2005), pp. 20–21, at: creationontheweb.com.

Vestigial organs and embryology

It is sometimes argued that organisms have organs and structures that are no longer used, indicating that evolution has resulted in their becoming non-functional. Perhaps the most commonly cited example is the human appendix, which was supposedly used in our evolutionary past but is now redundant. Other examples of 'vestigial organs' include the human thymus, male nipples and the small wings of flightless birds. Whales are said to have a vestigial hipbone, which was, allegedly, used millions of years ago, when their ancestors walked on land. Evolutionists also argue that the growth of vestigial structures can be seen in embryonic development. Some maintain, for example, that human embryos develop vestigial gill-slits because we were once fish, a vestigial yolk sac because we were once reptiles, and a vestigial tail because we were once monkey-like (see Fig. 27).

In order to clarify this issue, it is helpful to place each example of a 'vestigial organ' into one of three categories:

- those which were once thought to be non-functional but whose function is now known
- those which do appear to have no function, or may have a lesser function than in the past
- those which are, supposedly, seen in embryonic development.

The first category is the largest. The nineteenth-century anatomist Dr Robert Wiedersheim compiled a list of over a hundred organs that he understood to be vestigial, but since then, most, if not all, have been found to be functional. Professor Steve Scadding of Guelph University, Ontario, comments, 'As our knowledge has increased, the list of vestigial structures has decreased. Wiedersheim could list about one hundred in humans; recent authors usually list four or five. Even the current short list of vestigial structures in humans is questionable … I conclude that "vestigial organs" provide no special evidence for the theory of evolution.'[1]

Rather than being a redundant organ, the human appendix has been

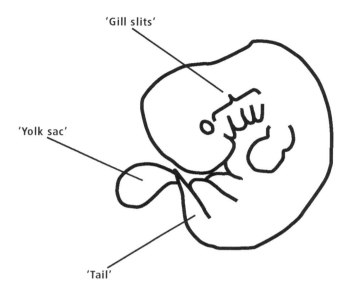

'Gill slits'

'Yolk sac'

'Tail'

Fig. 27 Human embryo with alleged gill slits, yolk sac and tail

found to be part of the immune system, preventing potentially harmful bacteria entering the small bowel from the colon. There is evidence that it is active in the production of antibodies and that its removal increases the likelihood of leukaemia and Hodgkin's disease.[2] It appears also to produce and store bacteria useful for the digestive system.[3] Such is the importance of the 'vestigial' thymus that it is now sometimes referred to as the 'master gland' of the immune system. It is necessary for the establishment of an effective immune system in childhood and also for restoring this in adults if it gets damaged.[4] The reason why male mammals have nipples is that the early forms of both male and female embryos have characteristics of both sexes; just as belly buttons are a remnant of early development, so are male nipples. Moreover, these are not without function, as they can be involved in sexual stimulation.[5] The vestigial 'hipbone' of whales is, in fact, an anchor for muscles and organs used in digestion and copulation.[6] *In many cases, parts of organisms are said to be vestigial simply because scientists don't know what they do, rather than because it is clear that they have no purpose*. Indeed, the assumption that a particular organ is vestigial has, very often, simply delayed the discovery of its real function.

A more recent candidate for alleged biological redundancy supposedly arising from evolutionary processes is 'junk' DNA, sometimes referred to as 'non-protein-coding' DNA. When the human genome was first mapped, the role of only around 3 per cent of it was understood—that is, the genes responsible for specifying the structure of proteins. Many evolutionists concluded that much of the other 97 per cent had no function, believing this to have been used in our evolutionary past but now discarded and corrupted by millions of years of mutations. As our understanding of genetics has grown, however, the proportion of DNA which might be considered to be 'junk' has reduced significantly.7 We now know, for example, that 'non-protein-coding' DNA is used for the regulation, maintenance and even reprogramming of genetic processes. Significantly, recent research suggests that the 'non-protein-coding' DNA regions are used more than the 'protein-coding' regions.8 According to Dr John Greally of the Albert Einstein College of Medicine, New York, 'It would now take a very brave person to call non-coding DNA junk.'9

Perhaps the best example of the second category (those which do appear to have no function, or may have a lesser function than in the past) is the wings of flightless birds, as it may well be that the ancestors of these creatures did fly. Similarly, evolutionists point to the existence of animals that live continually in caves which have incomplete or non-functioning eyes and are blind. Such cases do not demonstrate *e*volution, however, but *d*evolution—that functions can be lost. To demonstrate evolution, it is necessary to show that organs can be created through natural processes, not that they can become redundant. These conditions have probably arisen due to mutations which have resulted in *losses* of genetic information and do not, therefore, illustrate the central principle of evolution, this being the progressive *gain* of information and associated *increase* in complexity. The presence of the few organs that do genuinely appear to be non-functional is more consistent with a biblical view of 'the fall', whereby the originally perfect bodies given by God to animals (and Adam and Eve) have degenerated due to the effects of sin and a changed environment.

The third category of 'vestigial organs' (those supposedly seen in embryonic development) exists because of the tendency to associate superficial resemblance with biological relationship, an error that has already been discussed in Chapter 4 (Homology). In fact, embryonic human 'gill-slits' are not slits or openings and are more properly named *pharyngeal clefts* or *grooves*. They are simply the regions between the pharyngeal arches (Fig. 28). According to Professor de Beer, these clefts 'bear little resemblance to the gill-slits of the adult fish. Anyone who can see can convince himself of the truth of this.'[10] Moreover, these embryonic parts do not at any point develop into anything resembling gills (or lungs) but into the neck, throat, face and ear, and the thymus, thyroid and parathyroid glands. The human 'yolk sac' does not contain yolk, but provides the embryo with germ cells (which later become the man or woman's own sperm or eggs) and blood stem cells. Humans do not have a vestigial tailbone, but a coccyx—a structure used as an anchor for the gluteus maximus, a muscle needed for our upright posture and for the control of defecation and childbirth. Referring to the surgical removal of the coccyx, Dr Evan Shute FRCSC comments, 'Take

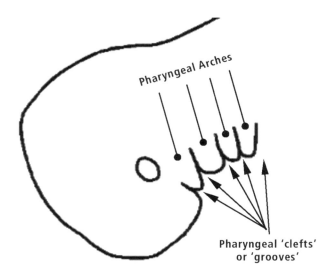

Fig. 28 Pharyngeal arches and pharyngeal 'clefts' or 'grooves'

it away, and patients complain; indeed the operation for its removal has time and again fallen into disrepute.'[11]

Some whale embryos develop teeth which disappear before birth and which are therefore argued to have no function and to be an evolutionary vestige. However, they do have a function, as they play an important role in the forming of the jawbone. The teeth (which do not at any stage pierce the gums) guide the development of the jaw, determining its length, and are then completely absorbed into the bone structure.[12] Unborn whales are also known to develop rear limb buds, which are then absorbed as the foetus continues to develop. In both cases it is possible that these creatures are descended from whales that once had teeth or hind limbs. But, again, this is devolution, not evolution. Moreover, this can be argued to be evidence of the genetic potential for variation within a created kind, with which God created the original animals.[13]

Other alleged embryological evidence for evolution has, historically, taken two forms. The first is that, as they grow, embryos supposedly pass through forms similar to those of their adult evolutionary ancestors. The second is much less sweeping, arguing, usually of vertebrates, that embryos of different species pass through a 'phylotypic' or 'conserved' stage, when they are virtually identical, before acquiring their final, diverse forms.

The first argument is variously referred to as *embryonic recapitulation*, the *biogenetic law* and *ontogeny recapitulates phylogeny*.[14] According to this, a human embryo supposedly begins in worm-like form, then becomes fish-like, then amphibian-like, then reptilian-like, before finally taking human form. The idea was popularized in the nineteenth century by the German evolutionist Ernst Haeckel, who even produced drawings of embryos apparently giving strong support to the theory. According to Professor Gould, due to Haeckel's considerable influence among the scientific community, his theory 'quickly became the common property of all evolutionists' and played 'a fundamental role in a host of diverse disciplines'. Indeed, it 'served as the organizing idea for generations of work in comparative embryology, physiology and morphology' and, well into the twentieth century, strongly influenced fields as wide-ranging as palaeontology, criminal anthropology, child development, primary education and psychoanalysis.[15]

The drawings upon which Haeckel made the case for his 'biogenetic law', however, were subsequently shown to differ from real embryos to such an extent that some regarded them as an act of deliberate fraud (Figs 29 and 30).[16] Support for this view was provided by the embryologist Professor Michael Richardson of the Department of Integrative Zoology, Leiden University:

The core scientific issue remains unchanged: Haeckel's drawings of 1874 are substantially fabricated. In support of this view, I note that his oldest 'fish' image is made up of bits and pieces from different animals—some of them mythical. It is not unreasonable to characterize this as 'faking' … Sadly, it is the discredited 1874 drawings that are used in so many British and American biology textbooks today.[17]

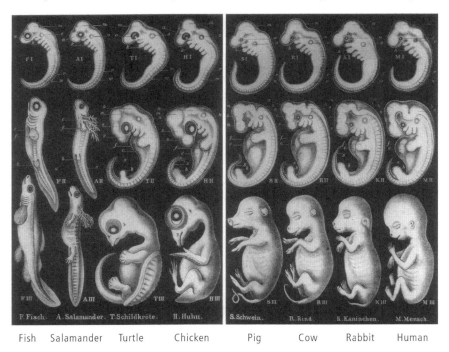

Fish   Salamander   Turtle   Chicken   Pig   Cow   Rabbit   Human

Fig. 29 Haeckel's fraudulent drawings of embryonic development
Note the similarities between the early stages.

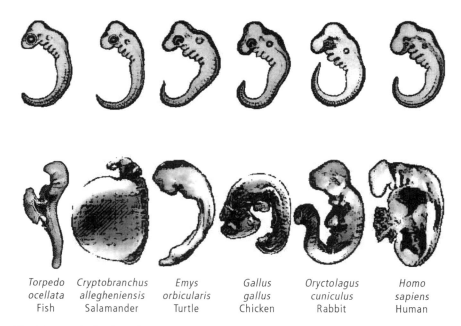

Torpedo ocellata	Cryptobranchus allegheniensis	Emys orbicularis	Gallus gallus	Oryctolagus cuniculus	Homo sapiens
Fish	Salamander	Turtle	Chicken	Rabbit	Human

Fig. 30 Haeckel's drawings compared with actual photographs
From Michael Richardson et al., 'There Is No Highly Conserved Embryonic Stage in the Vertebrates: Implications for Current Theories of Evolution and Development', *Anatomy and Embryology,* 196 (1997), pp. 91–106. © John Lewis 2009

Similarly, Professor Gould wrote, 'Haeckel had exaggerated the similarities by idealizations and omissions. He also, in some cases—in a procedure that can only be called fraudulent—simply copied the same figure over and over again.'[18]

Haeckel's 'biogentic law' has now been categorically rejected by virtually all modern evolutionary scientists. According to Professor Simpson, 'It is now firmly established that ontogeny does not repeat phylogeny.'[19] Similarly, the Yale University Biologist Professor Keith Thompson argued, 'Surely the biogenetic law is as dead as a doornail ... As a topic of serious theoretical inquiry, it was extinct in the [nineteen] twenties.'[20] According to Professor Gould, it has 'utterly collapsed',[21] and

Encyclopaedia Britannica describes it, quite simply, as being 'in error'.[22] In his book *Embryos and Ancestors*, Professor de Beer gives a number of reasons for the rejection of the 'biogenetic law':

- The order in which features appear in the embryo often differ from the accepted sequence of evolution. For example, teeth are understood to have evolved before tongues, but in the embryo, the tongue develops before the teeth.
- fossils understood to record the earlier forms of life, such as trilobites or brachiopods, are not similar in form to early embryonic stages.
- Early stages of embryonic development of closely related animals can be significantly different. In the case of velvet worms (*Peripatus*), two of their species are indistinguishable as adults but can be told apart as embryos.
- It is now known that, in their early stages, embryos possess features of their class, order, species and sex, as well as individual characteristics. Indeed, although not visible to the naked eye, the fertilized eggs of different animals are really as distinct from one another as are their adults.[23]

Modern techniques have enabled us to photograph human embryos perfectly, at every stage of their development, and show them to be quite unique.[24] Again, the order of development is sometimes opposite to the supposed evolutionary sequence: the tongue develops before the teeth, the brain before the nerve cords, and the heart before the blood vessels.

The second argument, referring to the 'phylotypic' or 'conserved' stage, however, is still current among many evolutionists. Professors Harry Butler and Bernhard Juurlink, for example, maintain, 'Embryos of different species [of vertebrate] pass through identical embryonic stages before acquiring their specific features.'[25] They are, of course, not *identical* at this stage, but it is true that, in many ways, some embryos are very alike in their outward appearance. The pharyngeal clefts referred to earlier, for example, are seen in the embryos of fish, reptiles, birds and mammals. However, because embryos reach these similar forms in such different ways, as we shall see, their similarities do not point to a common evolutionary ancestor.

Prior to their 'phylotypic' stage, these embryos are *radically* dissimilar, as

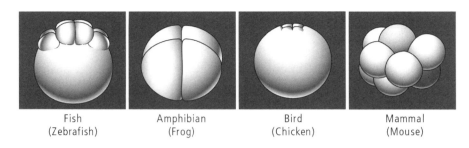

| Fish | Amphibian | Bird | Mammal |
| (Zebrafish) | (Frog) | (Chicken) | (Mouse) |

Fig. 31 Patterns of embryonic cleavage in different animal kinds. © John Lewis 2009

they pass through their *cleavage* and *gastrulation* stages. After fertilization, embryos undergo cleavage, in which the egg divides into hundreds or thousands of separate cells. The different vertebrate groups—mammals, birds, fishes and reptiles—cleave *very* differently.[26] Referring to the different patterns of cleavage, Lewis Wolpert, Emeritus Professor of

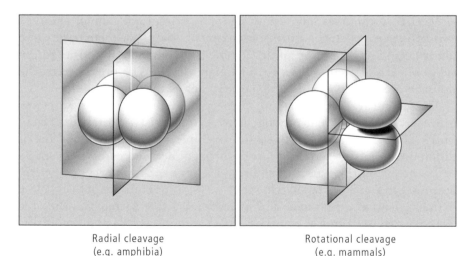

Radial cleavage
(e.g. amphibia)

Rotational cleavage
(e.g. mammals)

Fig. 32 Embryonic cleavage in amphibia and mammals
© John Lewis 2009

Biology at Kings College, London, comments, 'Nature seems quite profligate in the number of ways it has arranged for embryos to construct organisms. We may find unifying principles … but there is still much variety for which we have no explanation whatsoever.'[27] Some of these differences can be seen in Fig. 31. Particularly significant are the fundamentally different modes of cleavage. For example, in amphibia, the cells divide radially; in mammals, rotationally (Fig. 32). Referring to the differences between embryos following cell division, embryologist Dr Jonathan Wells comments, 'At the end of cleavage, the cells of the zebrafish embryo form a large cap on top of the yolk; in the frog they form a ball with a cavity; in the turtle and chick they form a thin, two-layered disc on top of the yolk; and in humans they form a disc within a ball' (Fig. 33).[28]

Following cleavage, embryos undergo gastrulation, when the cells rearrange themselves and establish the general layout of the animal's body. Such is the significance of this process that Professor Wolpert states, '… it is not birth, marriage, or death, but gastrulation which is truly "the important event in your life".'[29]

However, as explained by Dr Wells, 'Cell movements during gastrulation are very different … In zebrafish the cells crawl down the outside of the yolk; in frogs they move as a coherent sheet through a pore into the inner cavity; and in turtles, chicks and humans they stream through a furrow into the hollow interior of the embryonic disc' (see Fig. 33).[30]

Moreover, it has become clear in recent years that this 'phylotypic' stage is not as widespread as many have suggested. Professor Richardson comments, '… while many authors have written of a conserved embryonic stage, no one has cited any comparative data in support of the idea … [O]ur survey … does not support the claim and instead reveals considerable variability.'[31] This 'considerable variability' can be seen, for example, in Fig. 30.

According to embryologist Professor Erich Blechschmidt, who was Director of the Institute of Anatomy, University of Goettingen, 'The so-called basic law of biogenetics is wrong. No buts or ifs can mitigate this fact. It is not even a tiny bit correct or correct in a different form. It is totally wrong.'[32]

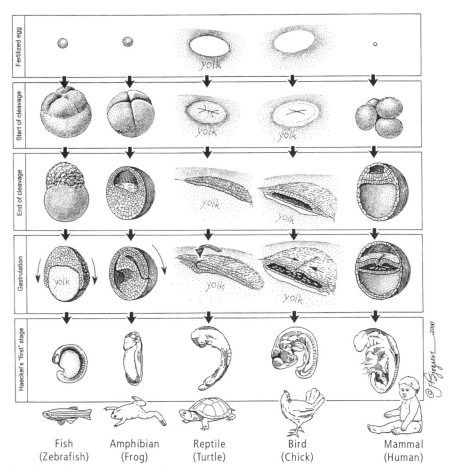

Fertilized egg
Start of cleavage
End of cleavage
Gastrulation
Haeckel's 'first' stage

Fish (Zebrafish)	Amphibian (Frog)	Reptile (Turtle)	Bird (Chick)	Mammal (Human)

Fig. 33 Early stages in vertebrate embryos

If fish, amphibia, birds and mammals all evolved from a common ancestor, why is their embryonic development fundamentally different?

Note: The fertilized eggs are drawn to scale relative to each other, but the scale of the succeeding stages are normalized to facilitate comparisons. © Jody F. Sjogren, 2000. Used by permission.

Notes

1 **Steve Scadding,** 'Do "Vestigial Organs" Provide Evidence for Evolution?', *Evolutionary Theory*, 5 (1981), pp. 173–176.

2 **Jerry Bergman** and **George Howe,** *'Vestigial Organs' Are Fully Functional* (St Joseph, MO: Creation Research Society Books, 1990), pp. 39–47.

3 'Purpose of the Appendix Believed Found', Associated Press, 5 October 2007; **R. Randal Bollinger et al.,** 'Biofilms in the Large Bowel Suggest an Apparent Function of the Human Vermiform Appendix', *Journal of Theoretical Biology*, 249(2007), pp. 826–831.

4 **Bergman and Howe,** *'Vestigial Organs' Are Fully Functional*, pp. 47–49.

5 **Jerry Bergman,** 'Is the Human Male Nipple Vestigial?', *TJ* (Journal of Creation), 15/2 (2001), pp. 38–41, at: creationontheweb.com.

6 **Bergman and Howe,** *'Vestigial Organs' Are Fully Functional*, pp. 70–71.

7 **Georgia Purdom,** '"Junk" DNA—Past, Present and Future, Part 1', *Answers*, 22 August 2007, at: answersingenesis.org.

8 **Alex Williams,** 'Astonishing DNA Complexity Demolishes Neo-Darwinism', *TJ* (Journal of Creation) 21/3, pp. 111–117.

9 Cited by **Andy Coghlan,** '"Junk" DNA Makes Compulsive Reading', *New Scientist*, 13 June 2007, at: newscientist.com.

10 **Gavin de Beer,** *Embryos and Ancestors* (3rd edn.; London: Oxford University Press, 1958), p. 52.

11 **Evan Shute,** *Flaws in the Theory of Evolution* (London, Ontario: Temside Press, 1961), p. 40.

12 **L. Vialleton,** cited by **Bergman** and **Howe,** *'Vestigial Organs' Are Fully Functional*, pp. 74–75.

13 **Kurt P. Wise,** *Faith, Form and Time* (Nashville, TN: Broadman & Holoman, 2002), pp. 219–220.

14 Ontogeny is the development of an individual organism from its earliest embryonic stage to maturity, while phylogeny is the evolutionary development of a species or group of organisms.

15 **Stephen J. Gould,** *Ontogeny and Phylogeny* (Cambridge, MA: Belknap-Harvard Press, 1977), pp. 77, 100, 116–117.

16 **Russell Grigg,** 'Ernst Haeckel: Evangelist for Evolution and Apostle of Deceit', *Creation*, 18/2 (1996), pp. 33–36, at: creationontheweb.com; answersingenesis.org.

17 **Michael Richardson,** 'Haeckel's Embryos, Continued', *Science*, 281/5381 (1998), p. 1289.

18 **Stephen Jay Gould,** 'Abscheulich! (Atrocious!)', *Natural History*, March 2000, pp. 42–49.

19 **George Gaylord Simpson** and **William Beck,** *An Introduction to Biology* (New York: Harcourt, Brace & World, 1965), p. 241.

20 **Keith Thomson,** 'Ontogeny and Phylogeny Recapitulated', *American Scientist*, 76 (1988), p. 273.

21 **Stephen J. Gould,** *Ever Since Darwin* (New York: W. W. Norton, 1977), p. 216.

22 'Haeckel', *Encyclopaedia Britannica*, vol. 5 (15th edn., 2005), p. 611.

23 **de Beer,** *Embryos and Ancestors*, pp. 7–13.

24 **Sabine Schwabenthan,** 'Life Before Birth', *Parents*, 54 (1979), pp. 44–50.

25 **H. Butler** and **B. H. J. Juurlink,** *An Atlas for Staging Mammalian and Chick Embryos* (Boca Raton, FL: CRC Press, 1987), page facing Table of Contents.

26 **Scott Gilbert,** *Developmental Biology* (8th edn.; Sunderland, MA: Sinauer Associates, 2006).

27 **Lewis Wolpert,** *The Triumph of the Embryo* (Oxford: Oxford University Press, 1991), p. 49.

28 **Jonathan Wells,** *Icons of Evolution* (Washington DC: Regnery Publishing, 2000), p. 96.

29 **Wolpert,** *The Triumph of the Embryo*, p. 12.

30 **Wells,** *Icons of Evolution*, p. 96.

31 **Michael Richardson et al.,** 'There is no Highly Conserved Embryonic Stage in the Vertebrates: Implications for Current Theories of Evolution and Development', *Anatomy and Embryology*, 196 (1997), pp. 91–106.

32 **Erich Blechschmidt,** *The Beginnings of Human Life* (New York: Springer-Verlag, 1977), p. 32.

Biogeography

Biogeography is the study of the distribution of plants and animals throughout the world. From this, it is known that each of the continents has its own distinctive fauna and flora. In Africa, for example, we find rhinoceroses, hippopotamuses, lions, hyenas, giraffes, zebras, chimpanzees and gorillas. South America has none of these. Instead, it is home to pumas, jaguars, raccoons, opossums and armadillos. Marsupials are found in Australia and South America, but not in Europe. Such observations have led biogeographers to divide the world into six main faunal regions (Fig. 34). Similarly, six main floral regions have been identified (Fig. 35). Evolutionists claim that the most reasonable explanation for these biogeographic distributions is that the different animals and plants evolved separately, from ancestors that colonized different areas of the world thousands or millions of years ago. Further evidence for this is argued from the study of island biogeography. For

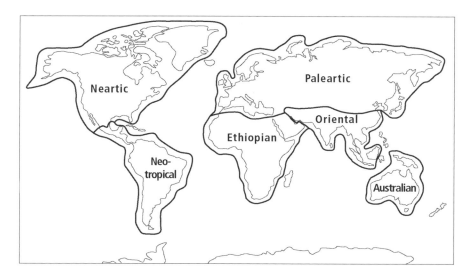

Fig. 34 Six major faunal regions

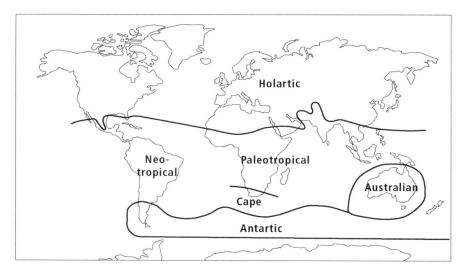

Fig. 35 Six major floral regions

example, of the 1,500 known species of fruit flies (*Drosophila*), nearly one third of them live only on the Hawaiian Islands. These islands are also home to more than 1,000 species of snails and other land molluscs that are not found anywhere else.

Here, again, it is necessary to differentiate between speciation *within* a kind (which is accepted as fact by both creationists and evolutionists) and evolution *between* kinds. Biogeography does indeed provide evidence in support of the former, and the fruit flies, snails and other molluscs found on the Hawaiian Islands arguably provide some of the strongest evidence we have of this. Similarly, clear biogeographic evidence exists for the speciation of finches around the Galápagos archipelago, where similar but different species are found on the different islands.[1] Almost certainly, this arose because the islands are close enough to enable a few birds to fly to a neighbouring island, but far enough away for the new colony to be isolated from the original group and less likely to interbreed with it. But how well does evolutionary theory explain the more general observations of biogeography?

In fact, some biogeographic observations are extremely *difficult* to explain within an evolutionary framework. According to the theory of

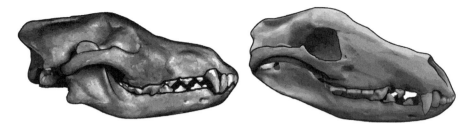

Fig. 36 Skulls of placental wolf (left) and marsupial wolf (right) © John Lewis 2009

evolution, mammals developed from small, shrew-like creatures around 100 million years ago. These creatures are argued to have evolved into, among others, the *marsupials* found in Australia and the *placentals* found in Europe and other parts of the world. What is so remarkable about these two groups is that, while their reproductive systems are fundamentally different, in other ways they are very similar. For example, the skeletal structures of some European placental dogs are almost identical to those of Australian marsupial dogs. This is particularly evident when the skulls of the Tasmanian marsupial wolf (*Thylacinus cynocephalus*) and the European placental timber wolf (*Canis lupus*) are compared (Fig. 36). Other placentals and marsupials, which supposedly evolved independently from one another, also show similar characteristics (Fig. 37). Is it really credible that *random* mutations and environmental conditions on *separate* continents could have given rise to such similarities?

Since evolution is argued as being a global phenomenon, it would be expected that new species would originate in many places throughout each continent. Hence, evolutionary theory would predict that centres of plant and animal dispersal would be randomly distributed, rather than concentrated in a few areas.[2] It has been known for many years, however, that this is not the case. As far back as 1820, Augustin de Candolle realized that the global pattern of plant distribution is closer to that of 'areas of endemism', where many different plants are confined to the same distinct and often small regions (see Fig. 41).[3] Subsequently, de Candolle's areas of high plant endemism were found also to correspond to areas of high animal endemism.[4]

Another problem for evolutionary explanations of biogeography arises because similar plants and animals are found not only across adjacent

Wolf
(*Canis*)

Wolf
(*Thylacinus*)

Ocelot
(*Felis*)

Native Cat
(*Dasyurus*)

Flying Squirrel
(*Glaucomys*)

Flying Phalanger
(*Petaurus*)

Ground Hog
(*Marmota*)

Wombat
(*Phascolonus*)

Anteater
(*Myrmecophaga*)

Anteater
(*Myrmecobius*)

Mole
(*Talpa*)

Mole
(*Notoryctes*)

Mouse
(*Mus*)

Mouse
(*Dasycercus*)

Not to scale

Fig. 37 Placental mammals (left) and their marsupial counterparts (right)
© John Lewis 2009

regions of land or neighbouring islands, but also on different continents, separated by large stretches of land or ocean. These are called *disjunct distributions*. Evolutionists sometimes explain these by arguing that continental drift separated similar groups that once lived in close proximity and therefore shared common ancestors (Fig. 38). This is the explanation given, for example, as to why chironomid midges are found in Antarctica, Southern Australia, South America, New Zealand and South Africa.[5] However, according to evolutionists' own theories, many species that are disjunct across previously joined continents evolved after their separation.[6] For example, South America and Africa allegedly separated around 100 million years ago, but species of cactus, which supposedly evolved in South America around thirty million years ago, are also found in Africa. Similarly, the evolutionary accounts of the emergence of rodents found in South America and Africa do not fit the generally accepted timing of continent drift.[7] Many other puzzling disjunctions across these continents are known.[8] Moreover, disjunct species are frequently found on continents that never bordered one another. For example, many plants and insects are known to be disjunct across the Pacific Ocean.[9] The distribution of the plant genus *Clethra*, for example, is shown in Fig. 39. Interestingly, the opossum *Dromiciops*, found in Chile, is much closer to Australian marsupials than to other South American marsupials.[10]

There is an abundance of other biogeographic anomalies that do not fit the expected evolutionary pattern. For example, the fauna of central and southern Africa is closer to that of southern Asia than that of northern Africa,[11] and flora found in Madagascar is remarkably similar to that of Indonesia.[12] Crowberries (*Empetrum*) are found only in the more northern regions of the northern hemisphere and in the most southern regions of the southern hemisphere. Many closely related plants are found only in eastern North America and eastern Asia. A study conducted by the Illinois State Museum showed that 627 seed plant genera are common to eastern Asia and eastern North America, 151 of which are not found in western North America.[13] Significantly, some of the plants (and animals) found in eastern Asia and eastern North America are identical at the species level, indicating that the disjunctions occurred very recently (that is, within the last few thousand years). If these disjunctions had occurred millions of years ago, as

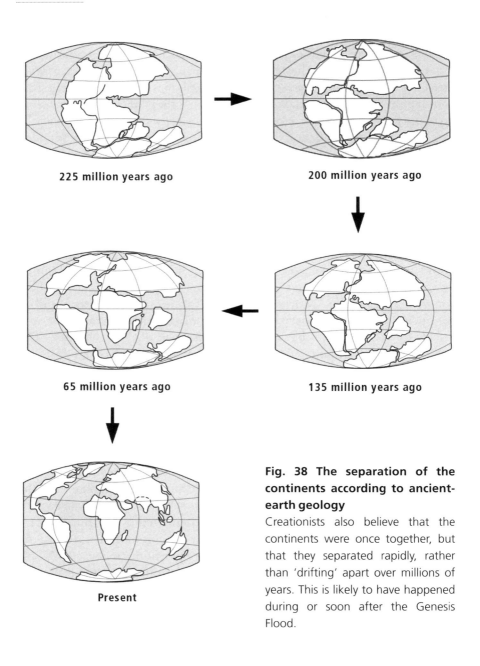

225 million years ago

200 million years ago

65 million years ago

135 million years ago

Present

Fig. 38 The separation of the continents according to ancient-earth geology

Creationists also believe that the continents were once together, but that they separated rapidly, rather than 'drifting' apart over millions of years. This is likely to have happened during or soon after the Genesis Flood.

evolutionists believe, it is most unlikely that so many species would have remained the same in the two areas. This is because plants and animals are known to change rapidly in response to changes in their environments.

The fossil record also presents problems for evolutionary explanations of biogeography. For example, there are many similar plant fossils in western North America and eastern Asia, but, according to the account of continental drift preferred by geologists, these rocks were laid down when Alaska and Russia were separated by thousands of kilometres of ocean.[14] While living marsupials are very largely restricted to Australia and South America, their fossils from the period evolutionists call the 'Late Cretaceous' (allegedly between 85 and 65 million years ago) are found exclusively in Eurasia and North America. As noted by Richard Cifelli, an Associate Professor in the Department of Zoology at Oklahoma University, 'this geographical switch remains unexplained'.[15] Interestingly, fossil marsupials have now been found on every continent.[16] According to evolutionary theory, placentals evolved in the northern hemisphere and did not appear in Australia until around five million years ago. However, a recent discovery of what appears to be a

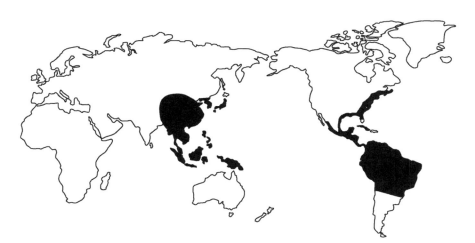

Fig. 39 Distribution of the plant genus *Clethra*
From Robert Thorne, 'Major Disjunctions in the Geographic Ranges of Seed Plants', *The Quarterly Review of Biology,* 47/4 (1972), p. 381.

placental fossil in Australia, in rocks supposedly 120 million years old, has caused evolutionists to suggest that placentals might have evolved first in the southern hemisphere, migrated north, and then become extinct in the southern continents![17] Lions are known to have lived in Israel, but fossils of lions have not been found there. Similarly, millions of bison once roamed the USA, but very few bison fossils are found there. To argue that a particular animal must have evolved in a particular place, simply because evidence that it lived anywhere else has not (yet) been found, is not necessarily scientific.

For these reasons, it is clear that the observed distributions of organisms cannot be explained simply by arguing that they evolved in the places they are now found. Consequently, evolutionists have supplemented their models of biogeography with alternative theories, such as migration across previously existing intercontinental land bridges, bird and wind transport, and transoceanic dispersal of plants and animals on floating vegetation mats.[18] In some cases, it is argued that distributions that are now disjunct were once continuous, and that plants or animals of these groups became extinct in the connecting land areas. Another theory proposed to explain puzzling biogeographic observations is 'convergent evolution'. According to this, different organisms evolved similar forms in different parts of the world as a result of having to adapt to similar environments. This is the explanation provided by evolutionists for the similarities between the placentals and marsupials in Figs 36 and 37, for example.[19]

In any discussion of patterns of biogeography it should be recognized that many of the theories are inevitably data-poor and, consequently, imagination-rich. The events in question all occurred many years outside of living memory and much of the evidence that might have supported any particular view may have disappeared long ago. It is perhaps significant that, in the nineteenth century, the case for an evolutionary interpretation of biogeography was based on a belief in separate, fixed continents, whereas now it is argued that the observed patterns of life support an evolutionary interpretation of biogeography based on continental drift. Perhaps the truth is closer to the view expressed by Drs Gareth Nelson and Norman Platnick of the American Museum of Natural History, who maintain, 'biogeography (or geographical distribution of organisms) has not been shown to be evidence for or against evolution in any sense.'[20]

Creationists, however, can turn to the Bible for clues in understanding the global distribution of fauna and flora. According to this, a recolonization of the world began immediately after the Genesis Flood, when the waters subsided (Genesis 8). The animals disembarked from the ark, and floating vegetation, carrying seeds, insects and freshwater fish, would have settled on the emerging land. Creationist models concentrate on four main processes which are understood to have influenced post-flood biogeography:

- transoceanic transport on vegetation mats
- transport by man
- migration and partial extinction
- speciation.

Transoceanic transport on vegetation mats

The potential for dispersal of plants and animals across large stretches of water by natural rafts has been accepted by evolutionists and creationists for many years. Professor Paul Moody of the University of Vermont argued,

In times of flood, large masses of earth and entwining vegetation, including trees, may be torn loose from the banks of rivers and swept out to sea. Sometimes such masses are encountered floating in the ocean out of sight of land, still lush and green, with palms, twenty to thirty feet [7 to 10 m] tall. It is entirely probable that land animals may be transported long distances in this manner. Mayr records that many tropical ocean currents have a speed of at least two knots; this would amount to fifty miles [80 km] a day, 1000 miles [1600 km] in three weeks.[21]

More recently, the rafting idea has been advanced by evolutionists to explain the presence of the Bear Cuscus (*Ailurops ursinus*) and the Dwarf Cuscus (*Strigocuscus celebensis*) on the island of Sulawesi[22] and of lemurs on the island of Madagascar.[23] In 1995, fisherman witnessed the colonization of the island of Anguilla in the West Indies by iguanas. These were washed up on one of the island's eastern beaches, having floated there on a mat of logs and uprooted trees, a few weeks after two hurricanes hit the islands of the Lesser Antilles. Scientists believed that the iguanas had rafted 320 km from Guadeloupe.[24]

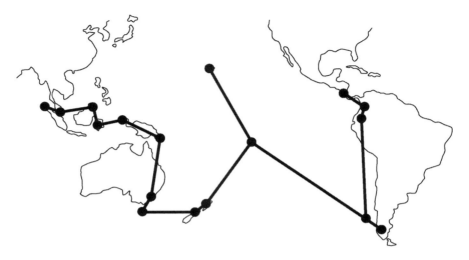

Fig. 40 *Oreobolus* track
From the Buffalo Museum of Science New York, USA.

Significantly, biogeographers sometimes refer to oceans rather than continents as the main biogeographic regions. This is because, very often, *patterns* of disjunction are seen where many terrestrial organisms are distributed around the land bordering an ocean. So clear was this to the twentieth-century biogeographer Léon Croizat that he spent much time drawing 'tracks' to chart repetitious occurrences of these patterns.[25] Where a particular track reoccurs in respect of different organisms, in group after group, it is often referred to as a 'generalized track'. The track for *Oreobolus* plants, for example, is shown in Fig. 40 and is one that is shared with a multitude of other plants and animals.[26] From these generalized tracks, Croizat identified five biogeographic 'nodes' or 'gates' of plant and animal dispersal across the world (Fig. 41).[27]

The destructive power of large volumes of fast-flowing water is enormous and, in the early stages of the Genesis Flood, would have been sufficient to rip up large amounts of woodland. Although some of this would have been buried in sediments, many billions of trees would have been left floating on the surface of the waters, as enormous 'log mats'. These islands of vegetation, regularly watered by rainfall, could have easily supported plant

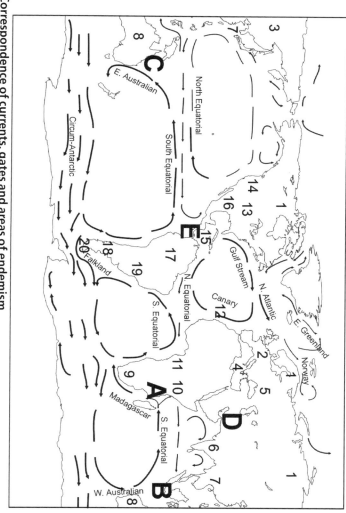

Fig. 41 Correspondence of currents, gates and areas of endemism

The twenty areas of endemism identified by de Candolle are indicated by the numbers 1 to 20. The five biogeographic 'gates' identified by Croizat are indicated by the letters A to E. From Kurt Wise and Matthew Croxton, 'Rafting: A Post-Flood Biogeographic Dispersal Mechanism', *Proceedings of the Fifth International Conference on Creationism*, pp. 465–477. Artwork by Stephanie Mace. Copyright 2003 by Creation Science Fellowship, Inc., Pittsburgh, Pennsylvania, USA. Published with permission. All rights reserved.

and animal life over significant periods of time. Ocean currents would have moved these massive 'rafts' around the globe, sometimes washing them up beside land, where animals and insects might 'embark' or 'disembark', and then transporting them back out to sea. The ability of ocean currents to distribute floating objects around the world was seen recently, when thousands of bathtub rubber ducks were lost off a container ship in the North Pacific in 1992. In fewer than twenty years, these had floated to Australia and South America, and subsequently into the Arctic and Atlantic oceans.[28] In support of the rafting theory, Professor Kurt Wise and Matthew Croxton point out that the intersections of ocean currents with land masses appear to correspond with de Candolle's areas of endemism and Croizat's biogeographic gates (Fig. 41).[29] It is not suggested here that land animals survived the Genesis Flood on rafts, but that rafts would have facilitated their dispersal after the Flood, as they multiplied and migrated away from the ark after it settled on mountains of Ararat (Genesis 8:4).

Transport by man

According to the Bible, following the dispersal of mankind at Babel (Genesis 11), the human race spread out over the *whole* of the earth.[30] Remarkable supporting evidence for this is found from archaeology, similarities in languages spoken by people in Europe and the Far East, and anatomical and DNA analyses.[31] It is reasonable to believe that many of these people, travelling to diverse regions, would have taken animals with them, as food for the journey and for subsequent farming on arrival at their destination.[32]

Migration and partial extinction

Many creationists believe that an Ice Age[33] followed soon after the Genesis Flood.[34] This would have lowered sea levels, as water accumulated as ice sheets, and could have created land bridges across which animals could migrate. Most evolutionists believe that a land bridge once existed across the Bering Strait, linking Asia with America.[35] Many geologists believe that there were major tectonic upheavals following the separation of the continents,[36] and land bridges that once existed in other parts of the world may have subsequently fallen below sea level. Animals could have migrated from one continent to another via these bridges, as they multiplied and spread out from the ark, perhaps over hundreds of years. The speed at which animals can spread by this process is demonstrated by the rabbits of Australia. Prior to the arrival of Europeans, rabbits were unknown on this continent, but, in 1859, a colony was introduced in Southern Victoria, in the south-east. Within fifty years, this had spread all the way to the west coast.[37]

It is clear that major changes in climate have taken place on various continents. Mammoths, rhinoceroses, bison, horses and antelopes, for example, once lived in large numbers in Northern Siberia. The deserts of Egypt were once rich savannahs.[38] Groups of animals that once thrived in certain areas could have become extinct in these places, and only those that migrated to other continents would have survived. Indeed, climate change and competition from other animals could well have *driven* migration. Alternatively, the absence of particular groups on particular continents can be understood to be because they never migrated or were never transported to these places and survived.

Speciation

Contrary to statements often made by those seeking to refute creationism, most creationists do *not* argue that species are fixed and cannot change. Rather, they argue strongly *in support* of the process of speciation. Apart from the strong scientific evidence in support of speciation, it is an essential component of the biblical explanation for the diversity of life now seen on the earth. According to the Bible, the only land animals that survived the Flood were those that were saved by Noah. Every kind of animal was represented on the ark; from these, all species now living must be descended (Genesis 6–8). Biblical creationists believe, in principle, that the genetic information necessary to produce all these species was carried by the animals that disembarked from the ark. It should be repeated, however, that biblical creationists do not believe that speciation can cross kinds, so a reptile would never 'speciate' into a mammal, for example, nor an ape into a man.

Accepting that animals and plants were made with the capacity to adapt to new environments, creationists argue that the presence of similar species or genera, in closely connected areas, can sometimes be explained by biological change.

Conclusion

While observations of biogeography provide strong evidence for the process of speciation, they do not support the more general predictions of evolutionary theory or the ancient-earth geologists' model of slow, continental drift. The data, however, can be seen to fit the biblical account of recolonization and diversification following the Genesis Flood.

A biblical history of life		
Genesis 1	c. 4000 BC	Creation of the universe and life on earth in six days. Creation of the first man and woman from whom the whole of the human race is descended.
Genesis 6–8	c. 2350 BC	Destruction of the ancient world by a global Flood. Plants were preserved on the surface of the waters and land animals on the ark. Most of the sedimentary rocks were laid down catastrophically during this time, burying many billions of plants and animals, now seen as fossils, including coal and oil.
		Recolonization of the world by plants and animals following the Flood, including rapid diversification of animals into the many species found on earth today. The animals that were saved in the ark possessed all the genetic information needed to produce all living species. Similarly, the people saved in the ark possessed all the genetic information needed to produce all the peoples now living.
Genesis 11	c. 2200 BC	Dispersal of the human race over the whole earth, and the establishment of new languages, tribes and nations.
	c. 2350 BC–1500 BC	The Ice Age.
	c. 2300 BC–Present	Continued diversification of plants and animals, using their inbuilt capacity to adapt to changing environments.

Notes

1 **Todd C. Wood,** *A Creationist Review and Preliminary Analysis of the History, Geology, Climate and Biology of the Galápagos Islands* (Eugene, OR: Wipf and Stock, 2005), pp. 108–125.

2 **Todd C. Wood** and **Megan J. Murray,** *Understanding the Pattern of Life* (Nashville, TN: Broadman & Holman, 2003), p. 192.

3 **Christopher Humphries** and **Lynne Parenti,** *Cladistic Biogeography: Interpreting Patterns of Plant and Animal Distributions* (2nd edn.; Oxford: Oxford University Press, 1999), pp. 21–22.

4 **Gareth Nelson** and **Norman Platnick,** *Systematics and Biogeography: Cladistics and Vicariance* (New York: Columbia University Press, 1981), pp. 368, 524; **C. Barry Cox,** 'The Biogeographic Regions Reconsidered', *Journal of Biogeography*, 28/4 (2001), pp. 511–523, at: interscience.wiley.com.

5 **Mark Ridley,** *Evolution* (3rd edn.; Oxford: Blackwell Science, 2004), ch. 17.

6 **Wilma George** and **René Lavocat,** *The Africa–South America Connection* (Oxford: Clarendon Press, 1993), p. 159; **Charles Davis et al.,** 'High-Latitude Tertiary Migrations of an Exclusively Tropical Clade: Evidence from Malpighiaceae', *International Journal of Plant Sciences*, 165 (2004; 4 Suppl.), S107–S121, at: people.fas.harvard.edu/~ccdavis/pdfs/Davis_et_al_IJPS_2004.pdf.

7 **George** and **Lavocat,** *The Africa–South America Connection*, ch. 9.

8 Ibid. p. 159.

9 **Robert Thorne,** 'Major Disjunctions in the Geographic Ranges of Seed Plants', *The Quarterly Review of Biology*, 47/4 (1972), pp. 365–411; Buffalo Museum of Science (New York), 'Panbiogeography: Pacific Basin Tracks', at: sciencebuff.org/pacific_basin_tracks.php.

10 **Michael Allaby,** 'Dromiciopsia', in *A Dictionary of Zoology* (Oxford: Oxford University Press, 1999), at: encyclopedia.com.

11 **William Beck et al.,** *Life. An Introduction to Biology* (3rd edn.; New York: HarperCollins, 1991), p. 1324.

12 **George Schatz,** 'Malagasy/Indo-Australo-Malesian Phytogeographic Connections', in **W. R. Lourenço,** (ed.), *Biogeography of Madagascar* (Paris: Editions ORSTOM, 1996), at: mobot.org.

13 **Hong Qian,** 'Floristic Relationships between Eastern Asia and North America: Test of Gray's Hypothesis', *The American Naturalist*, 160/3 (2002), pp. 317–332.

14 **Charles Smiley,** 'Pre-Tertiary Phytogeography and Continental Drift: Some Apparent Discrepancies', in **Jane Gray** and **Arthur Boucot,** (eds.), *Historical Biogeography, Plate*

Tectonics and the Changing Environment (Corvallis, OR: Oregon State University Press, 1976), pp. 311–319.

15 Richard Cifelli and **Brian Davis,** 'Marsupial Origins', *Science*, 302 (2003), pp. 1899–1900.

16 *Quantum*, ABC, 6 November 1991, cited in 'Focus: News of Interest about Creation and Evolution', *Creation*, 14/2 (1992), pp. 5–8; **Duane Gish,** *Evolution: The Fossils Still Say No!* (El Cajon, CA: Institute for Creation Research, 1995), pp. 178–183.

17 Tim Flannery, 'Forum: A Hostile Land—Could One Tiny Fossil Overthrow Australia's Orthodoxy?', *New Scientist*, 2116 (1998), p. 47.

18 George Gaylord Simpson, 'Mammals and Land Bridges', *Journal of the Washington Academy of Sciences*, 30 (1940), pp. 137–163, at: wku.edu; **Robert Thorne,** 'Major Disjunctions in the Geographic Ranges of Seed Plants', *The Quarterly Review of Biology*, 47/4 (1972), p. 375; **Aslaug Hagen,** 'Trans-Atlantic Dispersal and Phylogeography of Cerastium Arcticum (Caryophyllaceae) Inferred from RAPD and SCAR Markers', *American Journal of Botany*, 88/1 (2001), pp. 103–112.

19 Another remarkable example of 'convergent evolution' is the echolocation systems used by bats and whales, which, again, are believed to have evolved quite separately. That such similar and very sophisticated systems could have arisen through chance mutations stretches credibility a very long way (**Lee Spetner,** *Not by Chance* (New York: Judaica Press, 1998)).

20 Gareth Nelson and **Norman Platnick,** *Systematics and Biogeography: Cladistics and Vicariance* (New York: Columbia University Press, 1981), p. 223.

21 Paul Moody, *Introduction to Evolution* (New York: Harper & Brothers, 1953), p. 262.

22 Tom Heinsohn, 'A Giant Among Possums', *Nature Australia*, 26/12 (2001), pp. 24–31.

23 Ian Tattersall, 'Madagascar's Lemurs', *Scientific American*, (January 1993), p. 90.

24 Ellen Censky et al., 'Over-Water Dispersal of Lizards due to Hurricanes', *Nature*, 395 (1998), p. 556; **Carol Yoon,** 'Hapless Iguanas Float Away and Voyage Grips Biologists', *The New York Times*, 13 March 2008, at: nytimes.com.

25 Christopher Humphries and **Lynne Parenti,** *Cladistic Biogeography: Interpreting Patterns of Plant and Animal Distributions* (2nd edn.; Oxford: Oxford University Press, 1999), pp. 33 37; **Léon Croizat,** *Panbiogeography*, vols. 1, 2A and 2B (self-published, 1958).

26 Ole Seberg, 'Taxonomy, Phylogeny, and Biogeography of the Genus *Oreobolus* R.Br. (Cyperaceae), With Comments on the Biogeography of the South Pacific Continents', *Botanical Journal of the Linnean Society*, 96 (1998), pp. 119–195; Buffalo Museum of Science (New York), 'Vicariance Biogeography and Panbiogeography of the Plant Genus Oreobolus (Cyperaceae): A Comparison of Methods and Results', at: sciencebuff.org/panbiogeography_of_oreobolus.php.

27 Croizat, *Panbiogeography*, fig. 259, vol. 2B, p. 1018.

28 Peter Ford, 'Drifting Rubber Duckies Chart Oceans of Plastic', *Christian Science Monitor*, 31 July 2003, at: csmonitor.com; **Ben Clerkin,** 'Thousands of Rubber Ducks to Land on British Shores After 15 Year Journey', *Daily Mail*, 27 June 2007, at: dailymail.co.uk.

29 Kurt P. Wise and **Matthew Croxton,** 'Rafting: A Post-Flood Biogeographic Dispersal Mechanism', *Proceedings of the Fifth International Conference on Creationism* (Pittsburgh: Creation Science Fellowship, 2003), pp. 465–477.

30 In this, the Bible is emphatic. According to Genesis 11:8, '... the LORD scattered them from there over *all* the earth'; and again, in Genesis 11:9, 'From there the LORD scattered them over the face of the *whole* earth' (my italics).

31 Lawson L. Schroeder, 'A Possible Post-Flood Human Migration Route', *TJ* (Journal of Creation), 19/1 (2005), pp. 65–72, at: creationontheweb.com.

32 John Woodmorappe, 'Causes for the Biogeographic Distribution of Land Vertebrates after the Flood', *Proceedings of the Second International Conference on Creationism*, 11 (1990), pp. 361–370.

33 That is, they believe in one Ice Age, from around 2350 to 1500 BC. See **Paul Garner,** *The New Creationism* (Darlington: Evangelical Press, 2009), ch. 15.

34 Don Batten, (ed.), *The Answers Book* (6th edn.; Acacia Ridge, Queensland: Answers in Genesis, 2004), ch. 16.

35 Scott Elias et al., 'Life and Times of the Bering Land Bridge', *Nature*, 382 (1996), pp. 60–63.

36 Biblical creationists also believe that the continents separated, but not over millions of years. They understand this to have happened very rapidly, during or soon after the Genesis Flood. Dr John Baumgardner of the Los Alamos National Laboratory, USA, has produced a computer model of the Earth's mantle, and has shown that tectonic plate movement could have caused the continents to separate both spontaneously and very rapidly. The model also proposes a possible mechanism for a global flood (**Don Batten,** (ed.), *The Answers Book* (Acacia Ridge, Queensland: Answers in Genesis, 1999), pp. 151–156).

37 Carl Wieland, 'The Grey Blanket', *Creation*, 25/4 (2003), pp. 45–47.

38 Tony Fitzpatrick, 'Scientists Find Fossil Proof of Egypt's Ancient Climate', Washington University in St Louis, at: wustl.edu.

'It is recorded in DNA'

Evolutionists argue that, using genetics, it is possible to reconstruct the evolutionary history of an organism. In the case of speciation within a kind, it is indeed true that such perfect sequences of genetic change can be observed that the path of speciation can be mapped, as is the case, for example, with fruit flies (*Drosophila*) found on the Hawaiian Islands. However, when such claims are made in respect of the evolution of one animal kind into another, the case is much less convincing.

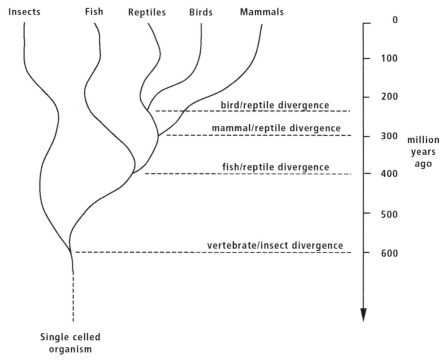

Fig. 42 Alleged evolutionary history according to the National Academy of Sciences

	Sequence Difference (%)	Supposed Divergence (million years ago)
Vertebrate/insect	24–34	600
Fish/reptile	16–30	400
Mammal/reptile	8–21	300
Bird/reptile	7–20	230

Table 1 Cytochrome C sequence differences between various animal kinds and the time at which they supposedly diverged from a common ancestor
From *Science and Creationism: A View from the National Academy of Sciences*, p. 19.

Evolutionists claim that, by comparing the genes of two living organisms that are understood to have diverged from a common ancestor millions of years ago, it is possible to measure the amount of evolution that has taken place. This can be done, they argue, by comparing the amino acid sequences of proteins, because these reflect the differences in the genes that specify their structure. In their publication *Science and Creationism*, the National Academy of Sciences compares a number of proteins found in various organisms. For example, they compare the amino acid sequence data of the protein cytochrome C found in insects, fish, reptiles, birds and mammals (see Fig. 42 and Table 1).[1] Since vertebrates and insects supposedly diverged from a common ancestor around 600 million years ago, and reptiles and fish diverged around 400 million years ago, they argue that one would expect to see a greater difference in the cytochrome C sequences when vertebrates are compared with insects than when reptiles are compared with fish. Similarly, since mammals and reptiles supposedly diverged around 300 million years ago, one would expect to see less difference in their cytochrome C sequences than when reptiles are compared with fish. Since this is what is found, the theory is argued to be sound and has given rise to the concept of the *molecular clock*. Hence, having estimated the rate of mutation for a given protein, the approximate date at which two organisms started to diverge from their common evolutionary ancestor can supposedly be calculated by comparing their sequences for this protein. A similar argument was presented in respect of haemoglobin.

A more critical consideration of this evidence reveals a different picture. The molecular clock hypothesis assumes a constant rate of mutation *per unit of time*, but observations show that rates of mutation are more meaningfully measured *per generation*. When one takes into account the different generation times of organisms, the theory is much less convincing. For example, the proteins of small rodents, such as mice, are no more divergent than those of primates, such as elephants or whales, which are species that have very much longer generation times.[2] The generation times of insects can vary by nearly one thousand times, but the proteins of different insect orders are equally divergent from those of vertebrates.[3] The generation time for fruit flies, for example, is around two weeks, whereas for cicadas it is seventeen years.

Moreover, the speed of the molecular clock appears to vary enormously when studied in different organisms and with respect to different proteins.[4] Evolutionary trees based on the molecular clock concept differ significantly from those produced by palaeontologists based on the fossil record.[5] According to Siegfried Scherer, Professor of Microbial Biology at the Technical University, Munich, 'A reliable molecular clock with respect to protein sequences seems not to exist … It is concluded that the protein molecular clock hypothesis should be rejected.'[6] These problems were confirmed more recently by Mark Farmer, Professor of Cellular Biology at the University of Georgia: 'We, as scientists, readily admit that our early approximations of using different genes for/as a stable molecular clock are probably flawed … quite simply, the molecular clock, when invoked to draw these types of comparison, is a flawed model sometimes, and it doesn't always work.'[7]

Regarding the expectations of evolutionists hoping to find in genetics the elusive proof of evolution and the 'missing links', molecular biologist Dr Michael Denton comments,

The prospect of finding sequences in nature by this technique was of great potential interest. Where the fossils had failed and morphological considerations were at best only ambiguous, perhaps this new field of comparative biochemistry might at last

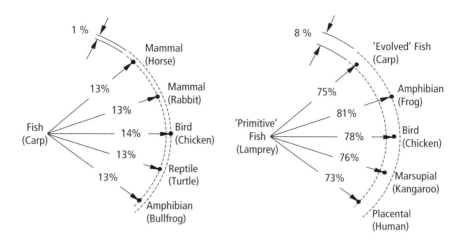

Fig. 43a Cytochrome C equidistance from carp

From M. O. Dayhoff, *Atlas of Protein Sequence and Structure.*

Fig. 43b Haemoglobin equidistance from lamprey

From M. O. Dayhoff, *Atlas of Protein Sequence and Structure.*

provide objective evidence of sequence and of the connecting links which had been so long sought by evolutionary biologists. However, as more protein sequences began to accumulate during the 1960s, it became increasingly apparent that the molecules were not going to provide any evidence of sequential arrangements in nature … all direct evidence for evolution is emphatically absent.[8]

Denton builds his case using data tabulated in Dayhoff's *Atlas of Protein Sequence and Structure*.[9] For example, he compares the cytochrome C sequence of a fish with that of an amphibian, reptile, bird and mammal. The differences vary by only 1 per cent, as shown in Fig. 43a, indicating that none is intermediate or transitional between any other. That is, while the sequences vary significantly between the various kinds (fish, amphibian, reptile, bird and mammal), as the National Academy of Sciences publication shows, when each kind is compared with the fish, the variation is seen to be negligible. Similarly, he compares the haemoglobin sequence of

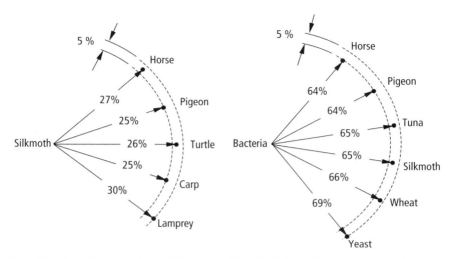

Fig. 43c Cytochrome C equidistance from silkmoth
From M. O. Dayhoff, *Atlas of Protein Sequence and Structure*.

Fig. 43d Cytochrome C equidistance from bacteria
From M. O. Dayhoff, *Atlas of Protein Sequence and Structure*.

a 'primitive' jawless fish (lamprey) with that of a 'more evolved' fish (carp), amphibian (frog), bird (chicken), marsupial (kangaroo) and placental (human), as shown in Fig. 43b. These differences vary by a maximum of only 8 per cent, with the human closest to the 'primitive' fish! Denton concludes, 'there is not a trace at a molecular level of the traditional evolutionary series, fish ⇨ amphibia ⇨ reptiles ⇨ mammals'.[10]

Hence, it can be fairly argued that studies of both cytochrome C and haemoglobin support neither the idea of the molecular clock nor the belief that some organisms are transitional or more evolved than others. In fact, the problem for evolutionists may be seen to be much worse when protein sequences of organisms with even greater differences in anatomy are considered, as explained by Dr Carl Wieland of Creation Ministries International:

… when you compare the amino acid sequence in the protein cytochrome C of a silk moth to that of the same protein in creatures as different from one another as horse, pigeon, turtle, lamprey, carp, all taken from Dayhoff's book, *Atlas of Protein Sequence and Structure*, they're all approximately the same percentage difference from the silk moth—between 25 and 30% [Fig. 43c]. That pattern seems to prevail everywhere. The distance from bacterial cytochrome to horse, pigeon, tuna, silk moth, yeast, wheat, is once again the same, 64–69% [Fig. 43d]. In turn, the horse cytochrome C is about the same distance from all the others. Every creature seems to be equidistant from every other creature on this basis. Of course, we are comparing today's bacterium with today's horse and the time from the alleged common ancestor would have been the same. So evolutionists have tried to explain away this unexpected pattern by saying that the molecular clock ticks at the same rate for all creatures … But all of them have greatly differing generation times. In one thousand years, bacteria go through vastly more generations than horses, say, and there are also not only countless more opportunities for copying mistakes, bacteria are actually known to have many more mutations per generation. This seems to suggest that most of the sequence differences did not arise by mutation and that the entire pattern fits the separateness of major groups of animals as per Genesis creation.[11]

Dr Wieland's final comment is extremely significant. Throughout nature, proteins exhibit a highly ordered pattern of diversity, with each class of organism isolated, distinct and unlinked by intermediates. This reflects not the predictions of evolutionary theory, but the biblical model—that God created different organisms according to their kinds, which have always been separate and unrelated groups.[12]

Notes

1 *Science and Creationism, A View from the National Academy of Sciences* (2nd edn.; Washington DC: National Academy Press, 2002), p. 19.

2 **Michael Denton,** *Evolution: A Theory in Crisis* (Bethesda, MD: Adler & Adler, 1986), p. 297.

3 Ibid. p. 298.

4 **Siegfried Scherer,** 'The Protein Molecular Clock: Time for a Re-evaluation', *Evolutionary Biology*, 24 (1990), pp. 83–105.

5 **Ernst Mayr,** *The Growth of Biological Thought: Diversity, Evolution and Inheritance* (Cambridge, MA: Belknap Press, 1982), p. 577.

6 **Scherer,** 'The Protein Molecular Clock'.

7 *Clash Over Origins*, debate between Dr Carl Wieland and Dr Mark Farmer at the Worldview Superconference, Asheville, NC, 2006. (DVD available from Creation Ministries International, Australia.)

8 **Denton,** *Evolution: A Theory in Crisis*, pp. 277–278.

9 **Margaret O. Dayhoff,** *Atlas of Protein Sequence and Structure* (Silver Spring, MD: National Biomedical Research Foundation, 1972).

10 **Denton,** *Evolution: A Theory in Crisis*, p. 284.

11 *Clash Over Origins*.

12 **Denton,** *Evolution: A Theory in Crisis*, ch. 13.

Part 3

The counter-argument in support of special creation

Evidence of design in nature

The evidence of a designer having been at work is not hard to detect. If we were to visit a desert island and see a sandcastle on the beach, we would immediately assume that an intelligent person had been there before us and built it. We would not assume that sand grains, randomly blown by the wind, had, by some freak of nature, fallen together in such a way as to form it. Why is this? Simply because the former explanation is so very plausible and the latter so very implausible.[1] The argument for there having been a designer behind life on earth, however, is by orders of magnitude more persuasive, because nature is so very much more complex than a sandcastle.

When Darwin looked down at a biological cell through an optical microscope, even at a magnification of several hundred times, what he saw appeared quite simple; modern microscopes, however, reveal a very different picture. According to Dr Denton, to do justice to the 'simple cell' we must

magnify it a thousand million times until it is twenty kilometers in diameter and resembles a giant airship large enough to cover a great city like London or New York. What we would then see would be an object of unparalleled complexity and adaptive design. On the surface of the cell we would see millions of openings, like the portholes of a vast spaceship, opening and closing to allow a continual stream of materials to flow in and out. If we were to enter one of these openings we would find ourselves in a world of supreme technology and bewildering complexity. We would see endless highly organized corridors and conduits branching in every direction away from the perimeter of the cell, some leading to the central memory bank in the nucleus and others to assembly plants and processing units … We would see all around us, in every direction, all sorts of robot-like machines. We would notice that the simplest of the functional components of the cell, the protein molecules, were astonishingly complex pieces of molecular machinery, each one consisting of about three thousand atoms arranged in highly organized 3-D spatial conformation … We would see that nearly every feature of our own advanced machines had its analogue in the cell: artificial languages and their decoding systems, memory banks for information storage and retrieval, elegant control systems regulating the automated assembly of parts and components, error fail-safe and proof-reading devices utilized for quality control … What we would be witnessing would be an object resembling an immense automated factory, a factory larger than a city and carrying out almost as many unique functions as all the manufacturing activities of man on earth. However, it would be a factory which would have one capacity not equalled in any of our own most advanced machines, for it would be capable of replicating its entire structure within a matter of a few hours.[2]

Can such complexity arise by chance processes?

But nature is not just complex—it is often *irreducibly complex*. This means that there are biological mechanisms that require a minimum number of parts in order to work, and removing just one part will result in total loss of function. A good example of this is the human knee joint, which engineers would describe as a four-bar mechanism (Fig. 44a–c and Table 2). Stuart Burgess, Professor of Design and Nature and Head of Department of Mechanical Engineering at Bristol University, made a detailed study of the knee joint and showed, as a conservative estimate, that it contains sixteen characteristics which are essential to its function. Unless the four-bar mechanism produces a sliding/rolling motion that is almost exactly compatible with the curved profiles of the upper and lower leg bones, the cruciate ligaments will not be kept under the right tension and the joint will not work. To achieve this, the shapes of the contact areas of the bones, the positions of the ligament-attachment points and the lengths of the ligaments must all be correct. As Professor Burgess concluded, it is impossible to argue that the knee evolved progressively because, until complete, it would have no useful function at all.[3]

Michael Behe, Professor of Biochemistry at Lehigh University, Pennsylvania, argues that there are many complex, irreducible mechanisms at the biochemical level that can only be explained by intelligent design. These include the biochemical activity within the eye, blood clotting, the immune system and transportation of proteins within a cell. In the case of blood clotting, for example, it is essential that proteins act in unison: the lack of one function would lead to the animal bleeding to death, whereas the lack of another function would lead to all its blood becoming one large clot.

Are there any explanations as to how complex biochemical systems could have evolved? Not according to Professor Behe:

Molecular evolution is not based on scientific authority. There is no publication in the scientific literature—in prestigious journals, speciality journals, or books—that describes how molecular evolution of any real, complex, biochemical system either did occur or even might have occurred. There are assertions that such evolution occurred, but absolutely none are supported by pertinent experiments or calculations. Since no one knows molecular evolution by direct experience, and since there is no authority on

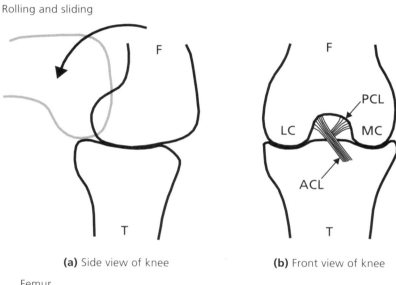

Rolling and sliding

(a) Side view of knee   **(b)** Front view of knee

F   Femur
T   Tibia
LC   Lateral condyle
MC   Medial condyle
PCL Posterior cruciate ligament
ACL Anterior cruciate ligament

Fig. 44a Anatomy of the knee joint (peripheral ligaments and knee cap removed)
Figs 44a–c and Table 2 © Stuart Burgess, *Hallmarks of Design*. Used by permission.

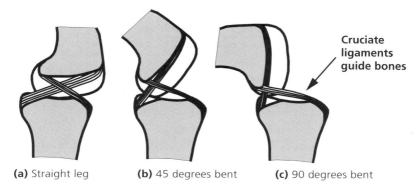

(a) Straight leg   **(b)** 45 degrees bent   **(c)** 90 degrees bent

Fig. 44b The irreducible mechanism of the knee (bones cut to show ligaments)

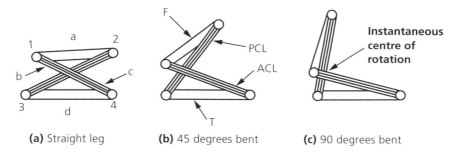

(a) Straight leg   **(b)** 45 degrees bent   **(c)** 90 degrees bent

Fig. 44c Schematic of the four-bar mechanism in the knee joint

Table 2 Essential characteristics in the knee joint

PART	ESSENTIAL CHARACTERISTICS	NO. OF CHARACTERISTICS
Femur bone	Protrusion of two condyles	2
	Convex curvature of two condyles	2
	Position of ligament attachment points 1 & 2	2
Tibia bone	Concave curvature of two tracks	2
	Position of ligament attachment points 3 & 4	2
Anterior cruciate ligament	Assembly of ligament to points 1 & 4	2
	Length of ligament	1
Posterior cruciate ligament	Assembly of ligament to points 2 & 3	2
	Length of ligament	1
	TOTAL	16

which to base claims of knowledge, it can truly be said that … the assertion of Darwinian molecular evolution is merely bluster.[4]

Some bacteria have motors that drive whip-like filaments (called flagella) that are used to provide locomotion.[5] In the case of the bacterium shown in Fig. 45, a number of flagella combine to form a helical screw propeller. These motors have bearings, rotors, stators, clutches and universal joints, can rotate up to 20,000 times per minute and reverse direction in one thousandth of a second.[6] They have been described by Harvard University biologist Professor Howard Berg as 'the most efficient machines in the universe'.[7] Can such things be built up over millions of years through thousands of small changes, each one conferring a benefit upon the organism? Apart from their obvious complexity, these mechanisms require many auxiliary proteins in order to function, for example, to turn the motor on and off, to assist in the assembly of the flagella and for the motor output shaft to penetrate the cell wall. As Professor Behe concludes, 'New research … cannot simplify the irreducibly complex system … The intransigence of the problem [of how this could have evolved] cannot be alleviated … Darwinian theory has given no explanation.'[8]

And there is more. As Professor Burgess argues, nature is not only incredibly complex and irreducibly complex, it is, from an evolutionary standpoint, *over-complex* or 'over-designed'. That is, it functions well beyond anything required for survival and cannot be explained by evolutionary principles such as natural selection and 'survival of the fittest'. For example, humans have the most remarkable ability to play musical instruments, which requires very specific functions of the brain and hands. What evolutionary process could have given rise to these? The prevalence of beauty in nature, generally, is a major problem for evolutionists. One example of this is bird songs. These include duets, matched counter singing (of one male to another), and, in the case of the blue jay, even the singing (simultaneously) of the notes of a major chord. Some birds have absolute pitch and nightingales have a repertoire of up to 300 songs. In speaking of the complexity and beauty of bird songs, William H. Thorpe, who was Professor of Animal Ethnology at Cambridge

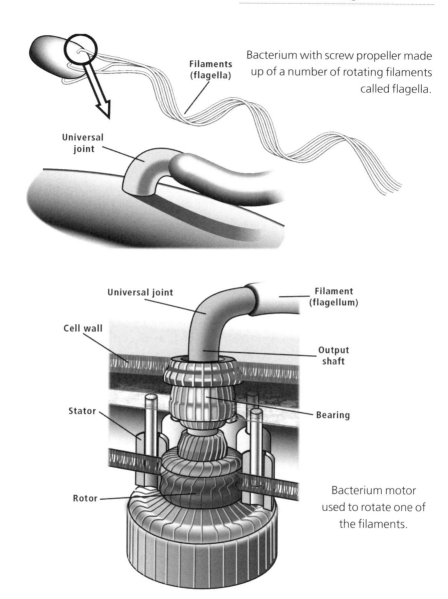

Bacterium with screw propeller made up of a number of rotating filaments called flagella.

Filaments (flagella)

Universal joint

Universal joint

Cell wall

Filament (flagellum)

Output shaft

Stator

Bearing

Rotor

Bacterium motor used to rotate one of the filaments.

Fig. 45 Bacterium with motors and rotating filaments which form a helical screw propeller. © John Lewis 2009

University, said, '… we do find a great deal of elaboration which goes beyond anything which would seem to be biologically advantageous … it is hard to imagine any selective reason for the extreme purity of some bird-notes.'[9]

And what about the information-storage system of DNA? The capabilities of modern computer systems pale into insignificance compared with this. The amount of information that could be stored in an amount of DNA with the same volume as a pinhead of 2 mm diameter would, if printed in a stack of paperback books piled one on top of another, reach a height five hundred times the distance of the moon from the earth.[10] The origin of the genetic code is again a most difficult problem for evolutionists. Sir Karl Popper, who has been described as 'incomparably the greatest philosopher of science that has ever been',[11] commented,

What makes the origin of life and of the genetic code a disturbing riddle is this: the genetic code is without any biological function unless it is translated; that is, unless it leads to the synthesis of the proteins whose structure is laid down by the code. But … the machinery by which the cell (at least the non-primitive cell, which is the only one we know) translates the code 'consists of at least fifty macromolecular components *which are themselves coded in the DNA*.' Thus the code cannot be translated except by using certain products of its translation. This constitutes a baffling circle; a really vicious circle, it seems, for any attempt to form a model, or a theory, of the genesis of the genetic code.

Thus we may be faced with the possibility that the origin of life (like the origin of the universe) becomes an impenetrable barrier to science, and a residue to all attempts to reduce biology to chemistry and physics.[12]

Furthermore, it has been shown that the DNA code, which has four different letters and uses three-letter words, is optimal in terms of information storage, translation and accuracy of information transfer.[13] Many other conventions could have been used, having different numbers of letters and/or different numbers of letters in each word. What is so remarkable about DNA having the optimum system is that it is very difficult to argue that random changes coupled with natural selection could have brought this about. This is because any changes to the code would be interpreted as a garbled message by the translator, and the organism would then be made with defective or useless proteins. It would be like changing the keys on a computer keyboard—the typist might correctly press the newly labelled keys to create a message, but the reader would have no idea what it meant because the printed letters in the words would have changed. The optimum choice of code is therefore strong evidence of a designer.

And what about the sonar system used by some bats? This can differentiate between ultrasound echoes only two to three millionths of a second apart, which means it can distinguish between objects just 0.3 mm apart.[14]

And what about the human eye? This is sensitive to a single photon (upon which it is impossible to improve) and has a dynamic range of ten billion to one, which is ten million times better than modern photographic film. Its data-processing power beggars belief, as explained by Dr John Stevens, who was Associate Professor of Physiology and Biomedical Engineering at the Playfair Neuroscience Unit, University of Toronto:

While today's digital hardware is extremely impressive, it is clear that the human retina's real-time performance goes unchallenged. Actually, to simulate 10 milliseconds (ms) of the complete processing of even a single nerve cell from the retina would require the solution of about 500 simultaneous nonlinear differential equations 100 times and would take at least several minutes of processing time on a [1985] Cray supercomputer. Keeping in mind that there are 10 million or more such cells interacting with each other in complex ways, it would take a minimum of 100 years of Cray time to simulate what takes place in your eye many times every second.[15]

More recently, it has been estimated that two human eyes can do more image processing than all the super computers in the world put together.[16]

And what about the human ear? This is sensitive to changes in air pressure of 10^{-10} atm, which is equivalent to the change in atmospheric pressure arising from a change in altitude of less than 0.001 mm. The eardrum can respond to movements of one-tenth the diameter of a hydrogen atom. What makes this even more astonishing is that the eardrum is living tissue that contains blood vessels. Consequently, at the same time as it is sensing these tiny movements, it is being bombarded by red blood cells orders of magnitude greater in size than a hydrogen atom. The noise filtration system required to remove the resultant interference defies description.[17]

The ability of evolution theory to explain the existence of even relatively simple biological structures is highly questionable. The claim that it can account for the multitude of highly complex systems seen throughout the biological world stretches credibility beyond all reason. The immensely sophisticated and sometimes irreducibly complex nature of the millions of different organisms that populate our planet can much more adequately be explained by intelligent design.

Notes

1 In fact, we instinctively recognize two characteristics: (1) that the sandcastle has a *complex* (improbable) form and (2) that it has a *pattern* or 'specified' form. In other words, it has *specified complexity*. This naturally leads us to conclude that an intelligent designer built it. Complexity is also recognized as being specified if it has *meaning* or *usefulness*.

2 **Michael Denton,** *Evolution: A Theory in Crisis* (Bethesda, MD: Adler & Adler, 1986), pp. 328–329.

3 **Stuart Burgess,** *Hallmarks of Design* (Leominster: Day One, 2004), pp. 11–15; Stuart Burgess, 'Critical Characteristics and the Irreducible Knee Joint', at: creationontheweb.com; answersingenesis.org.

4 **Michael J. Behe,** *Darwin's Black Box* (New York: Simon & Schuster, 1996), pp. 185–186.

5 **Howard Berg,** 'Motile Behavior of Bacteria', *Physics Today*, 1999, at: aip.org; Indiana University, 'Microscopic "Clutch" Puts Flagellum in Neutral', 19 June 2008, at: physorg.com/news133108054.html.

6 Some excellent animations of the working of a bacterial motor and the assembly of the motor, universal joint and flagellum can be viewed at: fbs.osaka-u.ac.jp/labs/namba/npn/index.html (go to 'Movies', 'Movement of the bacterial flagellum' and 'Assembly process of bacterial flagellum').

7 Cited in **Michael Ruse** and **William A. Dembski,** *Debating Design: From Darwin to DNA* (Cambridge: Cambridge University Press, 2004), p. 324.

8 **Behe,** *Darwin's Black Box*, pp. 69–73.

9 **William H. Thorpe,** *Bird-song: The Biology of Vocal Communication and Expression in Birds* (Cambridge: Cambridge University Press, 1961), pp. 63–64.

10 **Werner Gitt,** 'Dazzling Design in Miniature: DNA Information Storage', *Creation*, 20/1 (1997), p. 6, at: creationontheweb.com; answersingenesis.org.

11 **Beverly Halstead,** 'Popper: Good Philosophy, Bad Science?, *New Scientist*, 87/1210 (1980), pp. 215–217.

12 **Karl R. Popper,** 'Scientific Reduction and the Essential Incompleteness of all Science', in **F. J Ayala,** and **T. Dobzhansky,** (eds.), *Studies in the Philosophy of Biology* (London: Macmillan, 1974), p. 270.

13 **Werner Gitt,** *In the Beginning Was Information* (Bielefeld: Christliche Literatur-Verbreitung, 1997), pp. 94–95.

14 'Bats Put Technology to Shame', *Cincinnati Enquirer*, 13 October 1998, p. A4.

15 **John K. Stevens,** 'Reverse Engineering the Brain', *Byte*, April 1985, p. 287.

16 **George F. Gilder,** *The Silicon Eye* (New York: Atlas Books, 2005), p. 29.

17 **David Menton,** *The Hearing Ear and the Seeing Eye* (video from Answers in Genesis, 2003, at: answersingenesis.org/video/ondemand).

Part 4

Science or ideology?

Is belief in evolution necessary for scientific progress?

The idea that a knowledge and understanding of evolution enhances scientific progress is highly questionable. Philip Skell, formerly Professor of Chemistry at Pennsylvania State University, commented,

I recently asked more than 70 eminent researchers if they would have done their work differently if they had thought Darwin's theory was wrong. The responses were all the same: No. I also examined the outstanding biodiscoveries of the past century: the discovery of the double helix; the characterization of the ribosome; the mapping of genomes; research on medications and drug reactions; improvements in food production and sanitation; the development of new surgeries; and others. I even queried biologists working in areas where one would expect the Darwinian paradigm to have most benefited research, such as the emergence of resistance to antibiotics and pesticides. Here, as elsewhere, I found that Darwin's theory had provided no discernible guidance, but was brought in, after the breakthroughs, as an interesting narrative gloss.[1]

Similarly, Dr Marc Kirschner, founding chair of the Department of Systems Biology at Harvard Medical School, remarked, 'In fact, over the last 100 years, almost all of biology has proceeded independent of evolution, except evolutionary biology itself. Molecular biology, biochemistry, physiology, have not taken evolution into account at all.'[2] Some have even suggested that belief in evolution has impeded scientific progress. Heribert Nilsson, who was Professor of Botany and Director of the Swedish Botanical Institute at Lund University, argued,

The final result of all my researches and discussions is that the theory of evolution should be discarded in its entirety because it always leads to extreme contradictions and confusing consequences when tested against the empirical results of research …

Moreover: my next conclusion is that, far from being a benign natural-philosophical school of thought, the theory of evolution is a severe obstacle for biological research. As many examples show, it actually prevents the drawing of logical conclusions from even one set of experimental material. Because everything must be bent to fit this speculative theory, an exact biology cannot develop.[3]

According to Professor Louis Bounoure, former President of the Biological Society of Strasbourg and Director of the Strasbourg Zoological Museum, 'This theory has helped nothing in the progress of science. It is useless.'[4] According to Professor de Beer, Haeckel's recapitulation theory 'had lamentable effects on biological progress'[5] and, according to Professor Blechschmidt, it set back real scientific embryology a hundred years.[6] A good example of where evolutionary thinking has impeded medical progress is the belief in 'vestigial organs'. The functions of these were not understood for years because they were assumed to be vestigial and a by-product of our evolutionary history. In the case of the 'vestigial thymus', it led to the thymuses of children being subjected to radiotherapy, with tragic results. For many years, the tonsils were understood to be vestigial and were often removed in childhood; but it is now known that these are part of the immune system. Removing them results in a four-fold increase in the likelihood of developing Hodgkin's disease, for example.[7] Similarly, the belief in 'junk' DNA has delayed progress in understanding genetics. Surely, if 'molecules-to-man' evolution were true, we would continuously observe in nature a creative process of immense power, one that would have an enormous impact upon research and development—in chemistry, biology, medicine and agriculture. Instead, in real, practical science, it appears to be irrelevant.

Despite this, it is often argued that the teaching of creationism or 'intelligent design' in schools as anything other than 'religious myths' threatens scientific progress. The facts of history, however, tell a different story. According to Professor Stanley Jaki, the scientific era *began* as a result of the Christian belief in a Creator.[8] One of the early founders of modern science was the seventeenth-century astronomer Johannes Kepler. In his *Epitome Astronomiae Copernicanae* (*A Summary of the Astronomy of Copernicus*), he wrote of how his scientific work was driven by 'the highest confidence in the visible works of God', and often interspersed his reflections on scientific method with biblical quotations on the wisdom, power and glory of God.[9] Galileo wrote that 'the book of nature is a book written by the hand of God in the language of mathematics'[10] and referred to the divine Creator as a 'craftsman' and an 'architect', concepts which inspired him to conduct experiments so as to learn about God's creation. Believing the human mind also to be the work of this Creator, he confidently pursued his research in the expectation that the mind created by God was capable of understanding at least some of the rest of God's creation. According to Galileo, it was this Christian belief that the principles of the universe were fathomable that led Copernicus to postulate the simple theory that the earth revolved around the sun.[11] The seventeenth-century mathematician René Descartes, who is sometimes referred to as the 'father of modern mathematics', explicitly derived his understanding of the laws of motion from his understanding of God. In his *Le Monde* (*The World*), he argued, 'These two rules evidently follow from that alone, that God is immutable, and that acting always in the same manner, He produces always the same effect.'[12] According to Professor Jaki, for Robert Boyle, 'the doctrine and belief in the Creator represented the very foundation of sound reasoning about the world', and Isaac Newton 'most explicitly endorsed the notion of a Creation once and for all as the only sound framework of natural philosophy'.[13] In an essay written for the Royal Society, John Maynard Keynes said of Newton that 'he regarded the universe as a cryptogram set by the Almighty'.[14] Newton himself, commenting on his astronomical observations, wrote, 'This most beautiful system of sun, planets, and comets could only proceed from the counsel and dominion of an intelligent and powerful being.'[15]

That the faith of these and other creationists provided the basis for modern science was acknowledged by the leading anthropologist and historian of science, Professor Loren Eiseley:

… the philosophy of experimental science … began its discoveries and made use of its method in the faith, not the knowledge, that it was dealing with a rational universe controlled by a creator who did not act upon whim nor interfere with the forces He had set in operation … It is surely one of the curious paradoxes of history that science, which professionally has little to do with faith, owes it origins to an act of faith that the universe can be rationally interpreted, and that science today is sustained by that assumption.[16]

These men were true scientists, in the modern sense. Like creation scientists today, they regarded natural laws as descriptions of the way God upholds his creation in a regular and repeatable way. Inspired by this, they engaged in observation and experiment so as to understand and explain the universe in terms of testable mechanisms.

Rather than belief in creation frustrating scientific progress, it is clear that the faith of these early scientists caused their work to be directed in fruitful ways. In our opinion, the later rejection of the Christian faith by many, and the consequent secular pursuit of science, has led to the very opposite of this. Now enormous amounts of time and money are expended in attempts to explain the origin of the universe and of life, something which is probably outside the scope of scientific knowledge.

Notes

1 **Philip S. Skell,** 'Why Do We Invoke Darwin? Evolutionary Theory Contributes Little to Experimental Biology', *The Scientist*, 19/16 (2005), p. 10.

2 Cited by **Peter Dizikes,** 'Missing Links', *Boston Globe*, 23 October 2005, at: boston.com/news/globe/ideas/articles/2005/10/23/missing_links/?page=1.

3 **Heribert Nilsson,** translated and cited in **Werner Gitt,** *In the Beginning Was Information* (Bielefeld: Christliche Literatur-Verbreitung, 1997), pp. 105–106.

4 Cited in *The Advocate*, 8 March 1984, p. 17.

5 **Gavin de Beer,** *Embryos and Ancestors* (3rd edn.; London: Oxford University Press, 1958), p. 172.

6 Cited in **Joachim Vetter,** 'Hands and Feet: Uniquely Human Right from the Start', *Creation*, 13/1 (1990), pp. 16–17, at: creationontheweb.com; answersingenesis.org.

7 **Lawrence Galton,** cited in **Jerry Bergman** and **George Howe,** *'Vestigial Organs' Are Fully Functional* (St Joseph, MO: Creation Research Society, 1990), p. xi.

8 **Stanley Jaki,** *Science and Creation* (Edinburgh: Scottish Academic Press, 1986).

9 Ibid. p. 268.

10 **Rodney Stark,** *For the Glory of God: How Monotheism Led to Reformations, Science, Witch-hunts and the End of Slavery* (Princeton: Princeton University Press, 2003), p. 165.

11 Jaki, *Science and Creation*, pp. 276–279.

12 Cited in Ibid. p. 281.

13 Ibid. pp. 285, 287.

14 John Maynard Keynes, cited in **Stark,** *For the Glory of God*, p. 173.

15 Cited in **Dinesh D'Souza,** *What's So Great about Christianity* (Washington DC: Regnery Publishing, 2007), p. 97.

16 Loren Eiseley, *Darwin's Century: Evolution and the Men who Discovered It* (New York: Anchor Books, 1961), p. 62.

Why do so many scientists subscribe to the theory of evolution?

Over the past hundred years, tremendous progress has been made in scientific understanding, enabling us to send man to the moon, cure many diseases and design computers with breathtaking data-processing speeds. This leads many people to believe that scientists are equally competent in explaining the history and even the origins of life on earth; but this is not so.

To send man to the moon, to cure or prevent diseases and to design computers requires competence in *operational science*, that is, the understanding of natural laws which can be obtained through careful observation and experiment in the present. There are many people in research and development institutions all over the world who are very good at this, to which the success of operational science testifies. Attempts to understand the history of life, however, requires competence in *historical* or *origins science*, which is more akin to the work of a detective or forensic scientist. It is much more difficult than operational science, because often we cannot prove our hypotheses by experiment and we rely on assumptions. It is also much more difficult than forensic science because we receive no help from eyewitnesses, as the issues relate to that which happened so far outside of living memory.[1] We are therefore much less adept at historical science, to which the disagreement among scientists regarding fundamental issues and the constant, major revision of their theories testify. Professor Ager, for example, admitted, 'It must be significant that nearly all the evolutionary stories I learned as a student ... have now been "debunked".'[2] Similarly, William Provine, Professor of Biological Sciences at Cornell University, wrote, 'Most of what I learned of the field [of evolutionary biology] in graduate (1964–68) school is either wrong or significantly changed.'[3]

It is interesting to note the care taken by scientists when making statements about operational science, because they know that what they say can be subjected to test and, if wrong, falsified. They feel much freer to make statements about origins because, very often, no one can prove them wrong. Furthermore, due to the imprecise nature of origins science, it can be misused in the same way that some misuse studies of the history of mankind, selecting only that evidence which suits the ideology or political objective they wish to promote.

Historical science is inevitably data-poor and imagination-rich, and this is one of the reasons why creationists and evolutionists, using the same data and applying the same scientific principles, can reach opposite conclusions. The real difference between these two groups lies in their *interpretation* of the data, which is often determined by their *worldview*. Significantly, the ardent evolutionist and former Harvard University Professor of Biology Richard Lewontin states,

We take the side of science *in spite* of the patent absurdity of some of its constructs, *in spite* of its failure to fulfil many of its extravagant promises of health and life, *in spite* of the tolerance of the scientific community for unsubstantiated just-so stories, because we have a prior commitment, a commitment to materialism. It is not that the methods and institutions of science somehow compel us to accept a material explanation of the phenomenal world, but, on the contrary, that we are forced by our *a priori* adherence to material causes to create an apparatus of investigation and a set of concepts that produce material explanations, no matter how counter-intuitive, no matter how mystifying to the uninitiated. Moreover, that materialism is an absolute, for we cannot allow a Divine Foot in the door.[4]

The 'evidence' for evolution lies, not in that observed in nature or in the fossil record, but in the *presuppositions* of the secular scientific community. Firstly, science is defined as excluding the supernatural, being based on natural, predictable laws only. Secondly, it is argued that, although scientific knowledge is incomplete, it has the potential to explain everything. Hence, according to these two principles, it must be possible to explain how life emerged through natural processes. Some theory of evolution is the most scientifically appealing hypothesis, and any observation that can be interpreted as supporting it is readily accepted as evidence of its validity. Observations that appear to contradict the theory are set aside, in the expectation that further scientific progress will one day explain why they present no real problem. This thinking, however, is demonstrably unsound. Although the definition of science as relating only to natural processes is reasonable, the assumption that natural processes gave rise to all that we observe today is not, because it cannot be tested. And if a theory cannot be, or has not been, tested, it is not scientific.

The very real and severe problems associated with the idea that random events (with or without natural selection) could have given rise to evolutionary processes have been known for many years. Serious objections to the Neo-Darwinian Theory, for example, were presented by some eminent scientists at a symposium at the Wistar Institute, Philadelphia, as far back as 1966.[5] According to the chairman, the zoologist and Nobel Prizewinner Sir Peter Medawar, such 'objections are very widely held among biologists generally'.[6] In one of the papers, the mathematician Professor Murray Eden of the Massachusetts Institute of Technology went so far as to say, 'It is our contention that if "random" is given a serious and crucial interpretation from a probabilistic point of view, the randomness postulate is highly implausible and an adequate scientific theory of evolution must await the discovery and elucidation of new natural laws—physical, physio-chemical and biological.'[7] Such statements are a clear admission that, to hold to an evolutionary position, it is necessary to appeal to *unknown* science ('new natural laws'), because *known* science indicates that the current theories don't work.

In discussing the problem of the origin of life, Professor Davies speaks equally candidly: '... where did the very peculiar form of information needed to get the first living cell up and running come from? Nobody knows ...';[8] 'No known law of nature could achieve this ...'[9]

Many evolutionists simply believe *by faith* that these new scientific laws will one day be discovered. But is it really credible that natural laws capable of producing something as complex as the human brain, with its ten thousand million nerve cells, *each* of which puts out somewhere between ten thousand and one hundred thousand connecting fibres, are now unobservable? Have these laws temporarily or permanently disappeared?

According to the Nobel Prizewinner Harold Urey, who is famous for his work in seeking to understand the early evolutionary origins of life,

… all of us who study the origin of life find that the more we look into it, the more we feel it is too complex to have evolved anywhere … We all believe as an article of faith that life evolved from dead matter on this planet. It is just that its complexity is so great, it is hard for us to imagine that it did.[10]

Another reason why some subscribe to the theory of evolution appears to be peer pressure. Rodney Stark, Professor of Social Sciences at Baylor University, commented, 'My reluctance to pursue these matters is based on my experience that nothing causes greater panic among many of my colleagues than any criticism of evolution. They seem to fear that someone might mistake them for creationists if they even remain in the same room while such talk is going on.'[11] Any scientist who openly considers a view of origins other than that of evolution faces instant ridicule and, all too often, limited career prospects. In some scientific establishments, scientists face persecution and can lose their jobs if they openly question Darwin's theory.[12] Apart from the obvious and most serious implications for free speech, this can only be a major obstacle to establishing truth, because open discussion is essential to the process of reaching a right consensus.

Evolutionists argue that their theory is scientific because it is based on the application of natural laws, whereas creationism is unscientific because it is based on faith. In reality, evolution, because of the lack of evidence in its support, is also a faith, and it is also, in many respects, unscientific, because there are such strong scientific arguments against it. The theory of evolution is not derived from convincing evidence but from a commitment to finding an explanation for our existence based on natural causes. It is scientific only in the sense that it is a collection of scientific ideas from which it is hoped, one day, to build a credible scientific theory. The evidence that such an endeavour can ever succeed, however, is no more than an assumption.

From time to time, when I am speaking to someone about evolution and I start to present the scientific evidence against it, the person smiles (sometimes kindly, sometimes less kindly) and asks, 'How else, then, do you explain the fact of life on earth?' This question, I have found, very often reveals the person's real reason for believing in evolution—it is not that the scientific evidence has convinced him or her, but that the alternative (supernatural, special creation) is *assumed* to be absurd. It never seems to occur to that person that, logically, the Bible's explanation of life could be the correct one. Phillip E. Johnson, Emeritus Professor of Law, University of California, Berkeley, concluded,

... from my own personal experience, it is pointless to try to engage a scientific naturalist in a discussion about whether the neo-Darwinist theory of evolution is *true* ... To question whether naturalistic evolution itself is 'true' ... is to talk nonsense ... [For such people] naturalistic evolution is the only conceivable explanation for life, and so the fact that life exists proves it to be true.[13]

And for some, 'evolution is a fact' because 'it is a fact that there is no God'. Logically, according to them, life *must* have arisen through natural processes.

Notes

1 Christian creation scientists, however, can argue that an eyewitness account is available, as God has given testimony to his act of creation in the Bible.

2 **Derek V. Ager,** 'The Nature of the Fossil Record', *Proceedings of the Geologists' Association*, 87/2 (1976), pp. 131–160.

3 **William B. Provine,** 'A Review of Teaching about Evolution and the Nature of Science', *National Academy of Sciences*, 18 February 1999, at: web.archive.org/web/20040709130607/fp.bio.utk.edu/darwin/NAS_guidebook/provine_1.html.

4 **Richard Lewontin,** 'Billions and Billions of Demons', *The New York Review*, 9 January 1997, p. 31.

5 **Paul S. Moorhead** and **Martin M. Kaplan,** (eds.), *Mathematical Challenges to the Neo-Darwinian Interpretation of Evolution* (Philadelphia: Wistar Institute Press, 1967).

6 Ibid. p. xi.

7 **Murray Eden,** 'Inadequacies of Neo-Darwinian Evolution as a Scientific Theory', Ibid. p. 109.

8 **Paul Davies,** 'Life Force', *New Scientist*, 1 (1999), pp. 27–30.

9 **Paul Davies,** *The Fifth Miracle* (London: Penguin, 1999), p. 100.

10 Cited in **Robert C. Cowen,** 'Biological Origins: Theories Evolve', *Christian Science Monitor*, 4 January 1962, p. 4.

11 Rodney Stark, *For the Glory of God: How Monotheism Led to Reformations, Science, Witch-hunts and the End of Slavery* (Princeton: Princeton University Press, 2003), p. 176.

12 *Expelled: No Intelligence Allowed* (video; Premise Media Corporation, 2008), at: premisemedia.com; **Jerry Bergman,** *Slaughter of the Dissidents* (Southworth, WA: Leafcutter Press, 2008).

13 Phillip Johnson, *Darwin on Trial* (2nd edn.; Downers Grove, IL: InterVarsity Press, 1993), p. 123.

Is evolution compatible with Christianity?

A s I learnt more about the theory of evolution, it became increasingly apparent that, rather than being a view of origins which is scientifically driven, it is, very often, *ideologically driven*. Moreover, and of greater concern, it is not difficult to see that this ideology is essentially anti-Christian in nature. According to Adam Sedgwick, who was Woodwardian Professor of Geology at Cambridge University and knew Darwin well, this was so from the beginning. A year after the publication of the *Origin of Species*, Sedgwick wrote of this, 'From first to last it is a dish of rank materialism cleverly cooked and served up … And why is this done? For no other solid reason, I am sure, except to make us independent of a Creator.'[1]

According to Dr Croft, Darwin's family, shortly after his death, deliberately destroyed many of his writings in order to obscure his anti-Christian sentiments.[2] Speaking a hundred years after the publication of *Origin of Species*, the biologist Sir Julian Huxley FRS argued, 'Darwinism removed the whole idea of God as the creator of organisms from the sphere of rational discussion.'[3]

Professor Dawkins openly admits that he writes books about evolution in order to promote atheism. When asked about his reaction to the fact that most people in Britain believe in God, he replied, 'I am unhappy to be living in a society where I think the majority of people are deluded. I'd love to do something about it, which is why I write the books I do.'[4] According to Professor Stark,

… the battle over evolution is not an example of how 'heroic' scientists have withstood the relentless persecution of religious 'fanatics'. Rather, from the very start it has primarily been an attack on religion by militant atheists who wrap themselves in the mantle of science in an effort to refute all religious claims concerning a Creator—an effort that has also often attempted to suppress all scientific criticism of Darwin's work.[5]

Indeed, the battle to defend Darwinism is fought so fervently that even evolutionists are heavily criticized if they find fault with it. When evolutionist Richard Milton published his book *Shattering the Myths of Darwinism*, suggesting that an alternative theory of evolution is needed, Professor Dawkins responded by attacking the publishers 'for their irresponsibility in daring to accept a book criticizing Darwinism'.[6] Similarly, when in 1981 the British Natural History Museum opened an exhibition on Darwin's theory, their failure to present it as fact caused outrage. The museum's staff were not creationists but believed that Darwin's theory should be questioned. They suggested, for example, that 'the concept of evolution by natural selection is not, strictly speaking, scientific' and that 'it may one day be replaced by a better theory'. The reaction from some members of the scientific community was so strong that the exhibition had to be changed and all 'offending' material removed.[7] In September 2008, evolutionist Professor Michael Reiss had to resign his position as the Royal Society's Director of Education because he had expressed the view that children should be allowed to raise doubts about the theory of evolution in their science classes and discuss alternative views of origins.[8] In our view, the fervour with which some evolutionists attempt to silence all who would criticize or even question Darwin's theory suggests that either they have something to hide or they have another, non-scientific agenda (or both). Real scientists know that the critical evaluation of their theories is essential to scientific progress.

Significantly, even scientists who have no commitment to principles such as intelligent design express concern at the ideological nature of the theory of evolution. Nobel Prizewinner Professor Robert Laughlin, for example, argues,

A key symptom of ideological thinking is the explanation that has no implications and cannot be tested. I call such logical dead ends antitheories because they have exactly the opposite effect of real theories: they stop thinking rather than stimulate it. Evolution by natural selection, for instance, which Darwin conceived as a great theory, has lately come to function as an antitheory, called upon to cover up embarrassing experimental shortcomings and legitimize findings that are at best questionable ... Your protein defies the laws of mass action? Evolution did it! Your complicated mess of chemical reactions turns into chicken? Evolution! The human brain works on logical principles no computer can emulate? Evolution is the cause![9]

According to the late Edwin G. Conklin, formerly Professor of Biology at Princeton University, Darwinism rapidly became a religion. Writing in the first half of the twentieth century, he argued, 'The concept of organic evolution is very highly prized by biologists, for many of whom it is an object of genuinely religious devotion ... This is probably the reason why severe methodological criticism employed in other departments of biology has not yet been brought to bear on evolutionary speculation.'[10] Similarly, leading philosopher and historian of science Professor Marjorie Grene maintained, 'It is as a *religion of science* that Darwinism chiefly held, and holds men's minds ... The modified, but still characteristically Darwinian theory has itself become an orthodoxy, preached by its adherents with religious fervour, and doubted, they feel, only by a few muddlers, imperfect in scientific faith.'[11]

More recently, Michael Ruse, who was Professor of Philosophy and Zoology at the University of Guelph, Canada, commented,

Evolution is promoted by its practitioners as more than mere science. Evolution is promulgated as an ideology, a secular religion—a full-fledged alternative to Christianity, with meaning and morality. I am an ardent evolutionist and an ex-Christian, but ... the literalists are absolutely right. Evolution is a religion. This was true of evolution in the beginning, and it is true of evolution still today ... Evolution therefore came into being as a kind of secular ideology, an explicit substitute for Christianity.'[12]

For others, the theory of evolution is expressed as an absolute denial of Christianity and its fundamental precepts. Professor George Gaylord Simpson stated, 'Man is the result of a purposeless and natural process that did not have him in mind.'[13] Similarly, the sweep of Professor Provine's 'science' is breathtaking. According to him, the theory of evolution shows that mankind has no purpose, establishes atheism, removes moral absolutes, disproves the resurrection and denies the concept of moral responsibility:

Modern science directly implies that the world is organized strictly in accordance with mechanistic principles. There are no purposive principles whatsoever in nature ... There are no gods and no designing forces that are rationally detectable ... modern science directly implies that there are no inherent moral or ethical laws, no absolute guiding principles for human society ... when we die, we die and that is the end of us ... [F]ree will ... simply does not exist ... There is no way that the evolutionary process ... can produce a being that is truly free to make choices.[14]

Evolution, I contend, is an ideologically driven, materialistic philosophy, whose primary effect has been to remove from mankind the knowledge of God. Leading scientists today argue not only that the Bible is a book of myths and false ideas (having been proven to be wrong, for example, by the theory of evolution), but even that Christian thinking is damaging. Perhaps this is nowhere more apparent than in Professor Dawkins's recent television documentary, *Root of All Evil?*,[15] and his book *The God Delusion*.[16] In the USA, secular pressure groups have successfully campaigned to remove Christianity from schools (on the basis that it contravenes the constitutional requirement to separate church and state) and to ensure that evolution is taught as fact. Their effectiveness is illustrated by a recent case when lawyers in the employ of the American Civil Liberties Union (ACLU) were instrumental in winning a court action against the Cobb County Board of Education. In consequence, the Board was ordered to remove stickers from school science books which contained the following statement: 'This textbook contains material on evolution. Evolution is a theory, not a fact, regarding the origin of living things. This material should be approached with an open mind, studied carefully and critically considered.'[17]

What is so remarkable about this ruling is that it is clear that the wording contained absolutely no reference to religious belief. To groups like ACLU, the presentation of the theory of evolution as 'proven fact' is a powerful weapon in the battle for people's minds and in establishing a secular worldview. It persuades many that Christian thinking is outdated and that we should embrace a more liberal society, without the 'restrictions' of Christian morality.[18] Similar actions can be expected in Europe. In June 2007, a committee of the Parliamentary Assembly of the

Council of Europe published a report with a draft resolution entitled *The Dangers of Creationism in Education*. This argued that creationism is a serious threat to medical progress, 'human rights' and democracy.[19] A few months later, the resolution was passed, with only minor changes, by forty-eight votes to twenty-five, reiterating that 'creationism could become a threat to human rights'.[20] In October 2007, the Swedish government decided to 'crack down on the role religion plays in independent[21] state schools' by banning biology teachers from teaching creationism or intelligent design alongside evolution. According to the Education minister, Jan Björklund, this was so that children would be 'protected from all forms of fundamentalism'.[22]

According to the apostle Paul, 'God's invisible qualities—his eternal power and divine nature—have been clearly seen, being understood from what has been made, so that men are without excuse' (Romans 1:20). The magnitude of the cosmos, with its billions of galaxies brought into being simply by God's word, speaks eloquently of an omnipotent Creator (Genesis 1:14–15). The complexity of the plant and animal kingdoms are undeniable evidence of an omniscient Creator. The beauty of nature, music and the arts points to a beautiful and good Creator. At the same time, widespread suffering and death throughout the world proclaim that something has gone wrong, and we are forced to ask the question, 'Why has our Creator allowed this?' We may then turn to the Bible for the answers. The Bible teaches us that God made a perfect world and a perfect man and woman (Genesis 1:31). They did not have to work hard to survive, for the ground easily produced the food they wanted (growing food only became arduous after they sinned, as is clear from Genesis 3:17–19 and 5:29); and there would have been no carnivory by either people or animals (Genesis 1:29–30). There would have been no disease and no physical or emotional pain, for God created a paradise in which mankind was to live in great joy and harmony. Most importantly, we would not have grown old and died. But because of sin, because mankind turned away from God and towards evil, God's judgement came upon us. We now live in a harsh climate; we have wars, hatred, starvation, divorce and great unhappiness, and all of us will one day die. But there is also good news for those who will receive it. God sent his only Son, Jesus Christ, into the world to pay the price for sin by dying on a cross. After three days, God raised him from the dead so that all who accept Christ may receive forgiveness of sins and a new, godly life through him. God promises also to raise from the dead all who are in Christ—and to a life better than that given to Adam and Eve.

But the theory of evolution denies all this. According to this theory, the divine qualities of God are not seen in nature, as life on earth is the product of chance and natural processes. Rather than suffering and death being the result of sin, they were the means by which life developed, through 'survival of the fittest'. Rather than God creating something that was in every way good, as the Bible maintains, an environment of disharmony, strife and desperate competition prevailed from the beginning. According to this thinking, sexual immorality, ungodly aggression, pride, and ruthlessness are not the result of sin but of evolutionary forces and are natural. Before people were taught that 'evolution is a fact and the Bible is full of myths', they saw in nature undeniable evidence of a creator God. They respected the Bible and were taught about sin and the way of salvation, and it made sense. They were brought face to face with the real, historic Christ and many accepted him as Saviour and Lord. Furthermore, important Christian principles and doctrines have their foundations in a literal interpretation of Genesis; these include the doctrine of original sin (Genesis 3; Romans 5:12–19), Christian marriage (Genesis 2:20–24) and the reality of God's judgement (Genesis 2:17; ch. 6). If it is accepted that the Bible cannot be trusted in matters of history, people will inevitably question whether it can be trusted in matters of doctrine and morality. Indeed, the theory of evolution is manifestly opposed to Christian truth: it robs God of his glory, confuses the gospel, and undermines the didactic and moral authority of the Bible.

A natural reading of the New Testament would suggest that Christ accepted a literal interpretation of the Old Testament, believing, for example, in the historicity of Adam and Eve and the Noahic Flood (Matthew 19:4–5; Luke 17:26–27). Indeed, he asserted that 'the Scripture cannot be broken' (John 10:35) and that 'It is easier for heaven and earth to disappear than for the least stroke of a pen to drop out of the Law' (Luke

16:17). Why did he say these things? Surely it is because the matter of biblical authority is of vital importance.

The Bible is a most precious book. It teaches us the essential truths about God and ourselves and answers the most important questions of life. It tells us where we came from and what it is to be human. In it, we find our Creator's instruction manual, informing us how to live. It teaches us right from wrong and counsels us that we might avoid the many pitfalls of life. In understanding it, we learn to think rightly, even as God thinks, and come to know ourselves. Moreover, we can come to know God, his nature, his uncompromising holiness and the love he has for us. In finding him, we can escape the emptiness of natural philosophies and discover real meaning and purpose. But the path to this knowledge is narrow (Matthew 7:14), and truth is not easily grasped. It must be sought fervently (Proverbs 2:1–5) and is found only by those who follow its precepts fully (John 8:31–32). There can be no vacillation, as the commitment to Christ must be total. Those who doubt God's Word will be uncertain of the path and robbed of its glory. Only by wholeheartedly embracing the Bible can we 'Love the Lord [our] God with all [our] heart and with all [our] soul and with all [our] mind' (Matthew 22:37). But if we learn to cherish it, the Bible will become for us a source of eternal renewal. We can then feed on the Bread of Life (John 6:35), drink from the Everlasting Spring (John 7:37–39), and press on to discover 'the unsearchable riches of Christ' (Ephesians 3:8).

Notes

1 **John W. Clark** and **Thomas Hughes,** *The Life and Letters of the Rev. Adam Sedgwick*, vol. 2 (Cambridge University Press, 1890), pp. 359–360.

2 **Lawrence R. Croft,** *The Life and Death of Charles Darwin* (Chorley: Elmwood Books, 1989), p. 95. See also **Russell Grigg,** *Darwin's Arguments Against God*, 13 June 2008, at: creationontheweb.com.

3 Cited in **Sol Tax** and **Charles Callender,** (eds.), *Evolution After Darwin*, vol. 3 (Chicago: University of Chicago Press, 1960), p. 45.

4 Cited in **John Blanchard,** *Evolution: Fact or Fiction?* (Peabody, MA: Evangelical Press, 2002), p. 28.

5 **Rodney Stark,** *For the Glory of God: How Monotheism Led to Reformations, Science, Witch-hunts and the End of Slavery* (Princeton: Princeton University Press, 2003), p. 176.

6 **Richard Milton,** *Shattering the Myths of Darwinism* (1st edn.; Rochester, VT: Fourth Estate, 1997), Preface.

7 **Phillip Johnson,** *Darwin on Trial* (2nd edn.; Downers Grove, IL: InterVarsity Press, 1993), pp. 133–142.

8 **Michael Reiss,** 'Should Creationism be a Part of the Science Curriculum?', BA Festival of Science, 11 September 2008; **Lewis Smith** and **Mark Henderson,** 'Royal Society's Michael Reiss Resigns over Creationism Row', 17 September 2008, at: timesonline.co.uk.

9 **Robert Laughlin,** *A Different Universe: Reinventing Physics from the Bottom Down* (New York: Basic Books, 2005), pp. 168–169.

10 Cited by **William R. Fix,** *The Bone Peddlers* (New York: Macmillan, 1984), p. 211.

11 **Marjorie Grene,** 'The Faith of Darwinism', *Encounter*, 13/5 (1959), pp. 48–56.

12 **Michael Ruse,** 'How Evolution Became a Religion: Creationists Correct?', *National Post*, 13 May 2000, pp. B1, B3, B7.

13 Cited in **Johnson,** *Darwin on Trial*, p. 116.

14 Cited in Ibid. p. 127.

15 *Root of all Evil?*, Channel 4, January 2006, episodes 1 and 2.

16 **Richard Dawkins,** *The God Delusion* (London: Transworld, 2006).

17 Northern District of Georgia, Atlanta Division, Civil Action 1 02-CV-2325-CC, January 2005.

18 According to the US Traditional Values Coalition, ACLU is active not only in promoting the teaching of evolution in schools, but also in stripping America of its Judeo-Christian heritage, opposing censorship, defending pornographers and abortionists, and, under the banner of protecting free speech, supporting openly paedophile groups such as the North American Man–Boy Love Association. See: traditionalvalues.org/pdf_files/ACLU.pdf.

19 *The Dangers of Creationism in Education*, Council of Europe Committee on Culture, Science and Education, Doc. 11297, 8 June 2007.

20 'Council of Europe to Vote on Creationism', ABC News, 26 September 2007, at: abc.net.au; 'Council of Europe States Must "Firmly Oppose" the Teaching of Creationism as a Scientific Discipline, Say Parliamentarians', press release by the Council of Europe, 4 October 2007, at: assembly.coe.int.

21 Most independent Swedish schools are privately owned but funded by government grants.

22 'Creationism to be Banished from Swedish Schools', *The Local*, 15 October 2007.

ABSOLUTE PITCH

The ability to sing a given pitch (that is, frequency of note) without an external reference.

AMINO ACID

A building block of a protein. There are approximately twenty different amino acids used to build proteins.

ARCHIPELAGO

A group of islands.

BIOTURBATION

The mixing of sediments by organic activity, such as by plant roots, worms and the burrowing activities of shellfish.

BIPEDAL

Able to stand and walk proficiently on two feet.

CLASS

A taxonomic group below phylum and containing one or more orders, e.g. Mammalia (mammals).

DNA

Deoxyribonucleic acid. A nucleic acid that carries genetic information.

FAMILY

A taxonomic group below order and containing one or more genera, e.g. Canidae (dog family), including wolves, foxes, coyotes and jackals.

FAUNA

Animal life.

FLORA

Plant life.

GENE

A segment of DNA that is passed from one generation to the next and which contains information used to specify the form or function of the organism.

GENERATION TIME

The interval between the birth of an individual and the birth of its offspring.

GENETICS

The study of the transmission and variation of inherited characteristics.

GENOME

All of an organism's genetic information, as encoded in its DNA.

GENUS (PL. GENERA)

Taxonomic group below family and containing one or more species, e.g. *Equus* (including horses, donkeys and zebras).

GEOLOGICAL COLUMN

A vertical cross-section through the earth's sedimentary rocks, with the most recently deposited (therefore youngest) rocks at the top and the oldest, earliest rocks deposited at the bottom.

GEOLOGY

The study of the history of the earth particularly as recorded in rocks.

HALF-LIFE

The time taken for radioactive

material to lose half its radioactivity.

HEAT DEATH

The theoretical final state of the universe, when it has run down to a state of no thermodynamic free energy to sustain motion or life.

HOMOLOGY

Similarity in position and form of a particular organ or structure to that seen in other organisms, believed by evolutionists to be due to their being descended from a common evolutionary ancestor.

IGNEOUS ROCK

Rock formed from solidified lava (or magma).

INANIMATE

Not alive.

INVERTEBRATE

An animal without a backbone.

MACRO-EVOLUTION

Large-scale change in organisms resulting in new taxonomic groups such as families, orders, classes, etc.

MACRO-MOLECULE

A very large molecule, such as a polymer or protein, consisting of many smaller units linked together.

MAMMAL

A class of warm-blooded vertebrate animals characterized by a covering of hair on the skin and, in the female, milk-producing mammary glands for nourishing the young.

MARSUPIAL

A mammal, the female of which carries and suckles her young in a pouch at the front of her body until they reach a mature state.

MICRO-EVOLUTION

Evolution resulting from a succession of relatively small genetic variations that often cause the formation of new subspecies.

MORPHOLOGY

The study of the form and structure of organisms without consideration of function.

MUTATION

A change to the genetic structure of an organism.

ONTOGENY

The development of an organism from its earliest stage to maturity.

ORDER

A taxonomic group below phylum and containing one or more families, e.g. Carnivora (meat-eaters).

PALAEONTOLOGY

The study of the history of life as recorded in fossils.

PETRIFY

Change (organic) matter into stone.

PHYLOGENY

The history of the evolutionary development of an organism.

PHYLOTYPIC STAGE

A stage in embryonic development

at which some (vertebrate) species closely resemble one another. Evolutionists believe this to be due to their phylogenetic relationship.

PHYLUM (PL. PHYLA)

A taxonomic group below kingdom and containing one or more classes, e.g. chordata (the chordates).

PLACENTAL

A mammal whose young complete their embryonic development in the uterus, joined to the mother by a placenta.

POLYSTRATE

Passing through more than one rock stratum.

POPULATION GENETICS

The study of the inheritance and prevalence of genes in populations.

PRIMATE

An order of mammals including lemurs, tarsiers, apes and humans.

PRIMORDIAL

Existing before life began.

PROTEIN

An organic compound consisting of a chain of amino acids that have structural or function roles in organisms. Examples are haemoglobin (which transports oxygen in the blood stream) and keratin (the main structural constituent of finger nails, hair, feathers, hooves, etc.). The structure or function of the protein is dependent on the type of amino acid at each position in the chain. Only a tiny fraction of combinations of amino acids will give rise to a biologically useful protein.

RADIOMETRIC DATING

A method used to determine the age of a rock or mineral by measuring the proportions of an original radioactive material and its decay product.

RODENT

A mammal such as a rat, mouse or squirrel, which has teeth adapted for gnawing or nibbling.

SEDIMENTARY ROCK

Rock formed from sediments deposited by either water or wind.

SELF-REPLICATION

A process by which something makes a copy of itself.

SONAR

A method of echolocation used by animals such as bats and whales.

SPECIATION

The process by which new species arise.

SPECIES

The taxonomic group below genus, e.g. *Felis Catus* (the domestic cat).

STRATIGRAPHY

The branch of geology concerned with the order and relative dating of rock strata.

TAXONOMY

The classification of organisms according to their structure. Humans, for example, are classified as follows: Kingdom: Animalia; Phylum: Chordata; Class: Mammalia; Order: Primates; Family: Hominidae; Genus: *Homo*; Species: *Homo sapiens*.

TERRESTRIAL

Living on or in the ground.

TRANSOCEANIC

Crossing an ocean.

VERTEBRATE

An animal having a backbone or spinal column.

ZIRCON

Zirconium silicate.

Translation project

If this book has been helpful to you, you may wish to help us make it available to others. Many people have little or no access to creationist material because little or nothing has been written in their language. Consequently, we would like translate this book into other languages, and on a not-for-profit basis.

If you would like to make a donation towards this work, this can be done through the Biblical Creation Society* at the web address

www.biblicalcreation.org.uk/bcs_publications/trans_donate.html

The author will accept no royalty payments for copies translated in this way.

*The Biblical Creation Society (biblicalcreation.org.uk) is a UK-based Christian charity that advances and defends the biblical teaching on creation.

Index

Index

Index

Index

Index